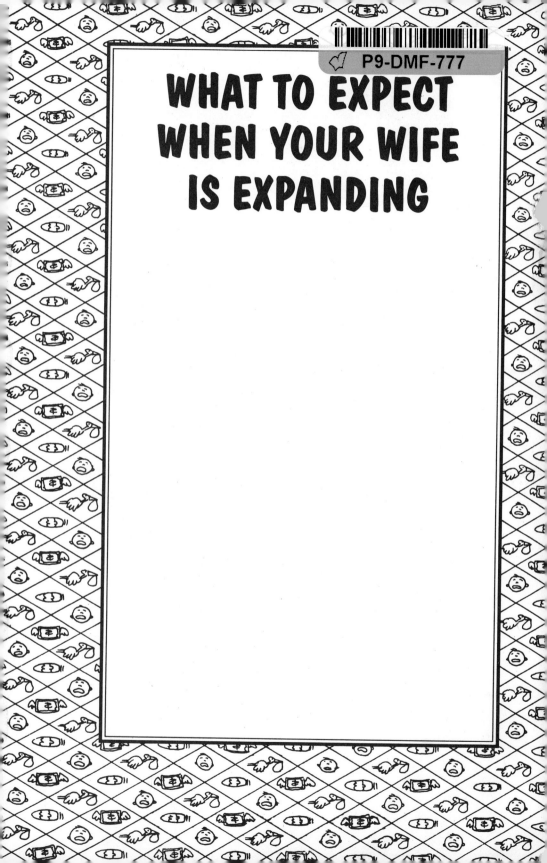

WHAT TO EXPECT WHEN YOUR WIFE IS EXPANDING

WHAT TO EXPECT WHEN YOUR WIFE IS EXPANDING

By Thomas Hill

Illustrations by Patrick Merrell

Cader Books

ANDREWS AND McMEEL
Kansas City

Produced by Cader Books
151 E. 29th Street
New York, N.Y. 10016

Cover illustration: Patrick Merrell
Book design: Cader Books

ISBN: 0-8362-8018-0

Library of Congress Cataloging-in-Publication Data

Hill, Thomas.
    What to expect when your wife is expanding / by Thomas Hill :
illustrations by Patrick Merrell.
        p.   cm.
    "Cader books."
    ISBN 0-8362-8018-0
    1. Pregnancy. 2. Childbirth. 3. Husbands. 4. Fathers.
I. Title.
RG525.H468   1993
    618.2'4--dc20   93-15734
                                                          CIP

First printing, May 1993.

2 3 4 5 6 7 8 9 10

DEDICATION

To my wife, Alison, for her love, wisdom, good humor, and unflagging determination—I don't know how I would have gotten through our two pregnancies without her.

ACKNOWLEDGMENTS

In appreciation for borrowed anecdotes and one-liners:
Simone Bloch-Wehba, Lou Collier, Michael Dignum, Katie Williams Fahs, Gretchen Friesinger, Rick Groel, Eleo Hensleigh, Larry Jones, Alan Kaufman, Suzanne Martin, Will McRobb, Conan O'Brien, Nina Silvestri, and Steve Slavkin. And in appreciation for the idea, a little pushing, and a lot of faith: Michael Cader.

CONTENTS

INTRODUCTION

It used to be so easy. The rabbit would die; only her doctor had to hear the monthly details. Dad took one frantic drive to the hospital, spent a few hours pacing, and *voilà!* Progeny! Pass out the cigars. Those were the days when every newborn came with an undebated last name.

Everything has changed. Good news for those rabbits, but not for the expectant father. And in case you're wondering, yes, not so many years ago laboratory technicians really did have to knock off a bunny for every single pregnancy test that came out positive. But we were talking about today's father. He has a dozen new roles: Lamaze coach, dietician, masseur, interior decorator, butler, psychotherapist, tugboat to her barge. Furthermore, he is expected to be well versed in all of pregnancy's medical details, options, and research, up to and including the current issue of *The American Journal of Obstetrics and Gynecology*, and should also be sensitive enough to know from across the room when the baby is kicking. All this, and he doesn't even get a healthy glow. What *about* the father? What about *his* needs, *his* problems, *his* concerns?

We set out to write *What to Expect When Your Wife Is Expanding* for every man who is facing fatherhood. It is the book we wished we could have turned to in our own moments of crisis, self-doubt, and, perhaps most of all, boredom. Everything you need to know about the next nine months is in the pages that follow, although of course you don't really "need" to know anything, except possibly that *psychoprophylaxis* is the scientific term for Lamaze training and does *not* mean birth control through mental telekinetics. And now you know that.

We have tried to be honest, factual, and reassuring. If, however, this book is generally terrifying, full of uneducated guesses, and peppered with reckless opinions, so be it. If we can make pregnancy easier for just one father, then it will all have been, well, actually, a complete waste of ink, paper, and man-hours. But if we can make pregnancy easier for just one hundred thousand fathers or so, then it will all have been worthwhile.

Our critics—that is to say, our wives—may say that it is only fair that up until now all the books have focused on the female experience of pregnancy. Women are doing all the real work, right? No matter how much you do as a pregnant Pop, nobody will ever practice kung fu on *your* spleen from the inside. Nobody takes over *your* body and soul for nine months. Isn't your wife doing all the real suffering? Isn't *she* the one who can't smoke one cigarette or have one beer and has to drink milk by the pailful and can't eat any foods she likes and is gaining tons of weight anyway, which is completely unfair, and doesn't even know how she will deal with the pain and is doing it all because *you* were so gung ho on starting a family?

And why do you need your own book? Why can't you just read all her pregnancy books and empathize? First, women don't understand how hard it is to empathize. Second, why should she begrudge you one lousy book. Third, her books are all really long and don't have very many jokes in them.

Is she the one who really deserves all the attention? Well, sure. But you'll be hearing all that from her. You've got a mate, but now you've also got *What to Expect When Your Wife Is Expanding*. This is the other side of the story. We'll never call you a thoughtless slug. We know that with all the new responsibilities and duties of being a father, you need guidance, information, moral support. We know it's hard to be an expectant father even when she doesn't. Remember, you're pregnant too! Just be selective about how often you tell her that.

A NOTE ON PRONOUNS

It is traditional in books like this for the authors to attempt to justify the use of the pronoun he when referring to a generic baby. Some say that it's just less confusing to have she mean mother and he mean the baby. Others find the he or she construction awkward. We are not so quick to bow to exigency and compromise.

Though it may take some getting used to, we chose to use an ampersand, slash, and dollar sign—&/$—to indicate the nominative he or she and a long row of eight asterisks—********—in place of the possessive his or her. Our only concession to gender stereotyping is that in almost all cases we will assume the pregnant mother is a she.

But then we changed our minds. (By the way, I will also be referring to myself as we, because it seems more authoritative.) The solution in the paragraph above is obviously unwieldy. Instead we will attempt to avoid the issue completely by avoiding as many pronouns as possible. We will call a baby a baby, and will use the grammatically incorrect their when we should say his or her: to wit, "When you first see your baby, you will want to nibble on their cute little toes." What do you want? Good grammar or gender neutrality? Furthermore, we may just slide into using him or her without even knowing it. Why are you reading this note anyway? Get to the text! You're having a baby, man, step to it!

CHAPTER ONE
What to Expect When "You're What?"

WHAT TO EXPECT WHEN "YOU'RE WHAT?"

Does life begin as "a gleam in father's eye"?

The idiom is outdated. Today, pregnancy is more likely to be planned, discussed, even scheduled. Couples consider their careers, their finances, their health, their age, the results of their genetic counseling, and current mortgage rates. Having a baby is complicated, expensive, and messy, yet people keep doing it. Scientists and sociologists suggest that this is largely because babies are so darn cute.

So a gleam in father's eye? Quite the opposite, old boy. In fact, pregnancy may still begin with gleam, but today that gleam is probably in her eye and she's not thinking about you, gorgeous. There comes a time in life when you're just the means to an eight-pound, two-ounce end.

There is, naturally, the possibility of simultaneous eye gleaming (and we all know how much fun that can be), which can mean either a pair of baby-crazy parents or a pair of very surprised parents who weren't expecting to be expecting. The former will probably invest in a wider variety of nursery wallpaper borders and baby books—but planners and non-planners both can be wonderful parents. Just because you're surprised doesn't mean you're not ready. Fate says you are, and the countdown to a new life—for you and the baby—started a month and a half ago.

Finally, there is the least common situation when the gleam actually is in the father's eye. When *you* really want to have kids and your wife has lingering doubts about dumping her career, sacrificing her body, and learning to love Barney and Baby Bop—that's *trouble*. Sure, you might talk her into it, but as the wait goes on, and the weight goes on—she'll know *exactly* who to blame. If you're eager to get started having babies, be very careful to make it seem like it was at least partly her idea. You might even want to get her to sign something.

No matter whose idea it is, so many joys and experiences lie ahead. Before you ever become a father, you're going to be "pregnant." You'll try to tape record the amplified heartbeat in the fourth month. You'll be parrying "Who's the father?" wisecracks from the boys. You'll nod knowingly, pretending you see it, while a doctor points at a piece of abstract art and claims that it is a sonogram image of Baby's head, spine, or "small parts."

You'll go along with your wife when she puts your hand on her tummy and says, "There, you had to feel that one." You'll debate the issue of paternity leave. Can you take it? And if you take it, can you take it? How long can anyone take it? You'll organize the Date-Weight-Sex Trifecta betting pools at the office for fun and profit, and if you're like the average man, you'll repaint the nursery 2.3 times before she likes the color.

You'll wonder about life with baby. Will you ever see your single friends again? And how will you explain that yes, you do need to go home even though yes, your wife is capable of watching the baby alone? How will you deal with problems of rivalry? What will happen when you and the baby vie for your wife's attention? Have you bonded with your baby? Why do they always pee the second the diaper is off? And how far does it have to go to be defined as projectile vomiting?

But let's face it. If you've read this far, you're probably a pregnant dad, or possibly a member of the author's family (hi, Mom! hi, Dad!), but in either case, you're committed. You're going to have to read the whole book. So go ahead. Take it one step at a time. This book will give you advice no other pregnancy book would give. That's a guarantee.

A NOTE TO THE MOTHER-TO-BE

We couldn't be more pleased that you are being supportive of your husband and reading *What to Expect When Your Wife Is Expanding*. Perhaps you're reading it because your husband was hiding it in his sock drawer. Perhaps you bought it for him—and want to make sure we're not out of line. Perhaps you've read every other pregnancy book you could find and are desperate. In any case, we're happy to have you here. Naturally, we are directing most of our comments to the father's experience, but you shouldn't feel left out. Understanding what your husband is going through is the most important thing you can do. And don't forget: Pregnancy can be just as challenging, rewarding, and involving for a woman as it is for a man. Good luck!

By the way, perhaps we should be more open-minded, and we're not about to climb on the family-values, Murphy-Brown-shouldn't-have-done-it bandwagon, but we feel strongly that a man shouldn't get pregnant on his own. Call us old-fashioned.

WHAT IT'S DARN IMPORTANT TO KNOW ABOUT PREPREGNANCY TESTS

Judging whether a woman is going to have a baby is a relatively simple matter of physiology. A home test or visit to a doctor can answer your question quickly and definitively. Judging whether a woman is in a state of prepregnancy is a much more difficult matter. However, it is important to know if such a condition exists. If she wants to have a baby, you should know about it. And vice versa.

The simplest test for determining prepregnancy is to listen to your wife. She will undoubtedly express her desire for a baby, if not directly, then in suggestive and leading comments: "Don't you think Zoe is a pretty name?" "Did you know there's a nice little nursery school just over on Elm Street?" or "My sister wants to know if we want Willy's crib now that he's out of it."

If listening to your wife is difficult, or if you never seem to know what she is getting at, it would be worth investing in any one of the many books on the market aimed at improving male-female communication. A few recommended titles: Mary Cornwall, *What Women Don't Tell Men But Expect Them to Know*, (Prentice-Schuster, 1989); E.P. Dunham, *Dictionary of the Female Language*, 15th edition, (Oxford Reference Books, 1985); Robin Filmoore, *I Am Listening, You're Not Saying Anything!*, (Freedentia College Press, 1992); D. Tanning, *You Just Don't Understand the First Thing About Women, You Ignorant Thick-Skulled Sexist Lout*, (Scott-Foreswoman, 1991).

If you don't have time to read up on communication, or even to take the Berlitz class, you still have the list below to help you make this important determination.

The early warning signs of prepregnancy:

Possible

▶ Suggests "sex."

▶ Bakes oatmeal raisin cookies more than once a week.

▶ Expresses new concern for your diet; recommends new vitamin pills for you.

▶ Suggests your study would make a nice bedroom.

▶ Tends increasingly to use pet names: calls you "Li'l Bear," the cat "Meowzi," her toothbrush "the brusherwusher."

▶ Shows extreme, even giddy interest in other people's babies.

▶ Renewed interest in real estate.

Probable

▶ Responds to your sexual advances by taking her temperature.

▶ Continues to use nicknames and now speaks in extended periods of baby talk: "Oh! 'itty Snuggums made all gone with his beer."

▶ Keeps forgetting birth control.

▶ Shows increased interest in the whole "stability" concept: pension plans, mortgages, dogs, neighborhood beautification projects.

▶ Starts knitting baby booties, or knitting anything.

▶ Stops drinking.

▶ Stops smoking.

▶ Stops swearing, to set a good example.

Definite

▶ Begins calling you "Daddy."

▶ Wants to make love twice a day for the three days around Thursday the twentieth.

▶ Says, "I want to have a baby."

▶ Throws away birth control.

▶ Paints and furnishes nursery.

▶ Says, "I said, I want to have a baby."

WHAT YOU SHOULD HAVE KNOWN BEFORE YOU BOUGHT THIS BOOK ABOUT HOME PREGNANCY TESTS

Rapid Response, FirstAlert, EPT Warning System. Not only is it difficult to choose from among the many home pregnancy testing kits that are available, but all three of these are actually home smoke alarms—and you don't want to come home with the wrong thing entirely. If you do, of course you can cover by saying that your plans to start a family have made you more safety-conscious, but you still won't know if the bun is in the oven. By the way, do not use the phrase bun in the oven until you have somehow ascertained that your wife does not have a virulent reaction to it.

The pharmaceutical companies have invested millions of dollars in the development of an accurate, dependable, and easy-to-use home pregnancy test. When these products first appeared on the over-the-counter market years ago, they were still untrustworthy, giving many false-positives, false-negatives, and occasional readings of "a negative times a negative is a positive," which is mathematically sound but leaves the pregnancy situation foggy. The early tests were approximately 75 percent as accurate as a good solid hunch.

Fabulous scientific breakthroughs, too complex for us to go out and actually do research on, have made these at-home tests remarkably accurate. Today, they are considered almost as reliable as a doctor's blood test, and who cares if your doctor is pregnant anyway? Let her buy her own pregnancy test.

Accuracy was achieved (at great expense, which you've probably noticed has been passed on to you, the consumer), but ease of use came more slowly. The early systems involved mixing chemicals, warming solutions, waiting for hours—and so left much room for error. Worst of all, no one could decide on the indicator. Should the little strip turn pink? Should the little ball turn blue? Should a little cartoon stork appear? Finally these scientific battles, too, were won.

Look for niche marketing soon. The division is too vast to straddle. Perhaps "Wild Thing" for the teen market, with the slogan "When ya gotta know right now, for sure." For the older crowd, something more high-toned: perhaps "Genesis" with the slogan "Be first to know." And of course both will boast, "Just hold it in your urine stream!" Now that's an appealing line of advertising copy.

What You May Be Concerned About
THE JOB OF SEX

"We're not pregnant yet, and yes, we know how it's done; but ever since we started trying to get pregnant, sex just isn't what it used to be. And we're still not pregnant."

Science has shown compelling evidence that sex is linked to pregnancy. So don't give up on this basic approach. Until there is new research, it appears that if you're going to have a baby, you pretty much have to do "it." This can be a complicated, tiring, and sometimes disorienting process, but don't forget that it can also be a loving and enjoyable one. Even fun, once you get the hang of it.

It may be hard to conceive, but for many couples, making the switch from recreational sex to procreational sex can be nerve-racking. Taking vitamin supplements, cutting down on caffeine and alcohol, checking the calendar, and taking her temperature are not traditionally thought of as foreplay. Subconsciously you may still have doubts about whether you are ready for fatherhood.

On the plus side, you are now working with the terrific advantage of not using birth control. (If you are still using birth control, that could be your problem right there.) In general, just try to forget about the ends and concentrate on the means. Think positive—after all, once you have a baby, you'll hardly ever have sex at all!

What You May Be Concerned About
EMOTIONAL MATURITY

"Am I ready for this?"

Sure you are. Well, all right, maybe you're not, but your wife is and she can help you out with the fine points of emotional maturity. Anyway, since you're reading this book, the question is moot.

If you are still having doubts, don't worry. Maturity isn't as complicated as psychotherapists would like you to believe. Becoming a mature, responsible, thoughtful, supportive, loving, giving, self-controlled, and self-aware person is really just a matter of behavior modification. Start with the list on the following page, find the immature behavior that you practice, and simply force yourself to choose the modified alternative. As you'll note, in some cases you don't even have to modify your behavior, just your explanation. After some initial backsliding, you'll find yourself behaving like a mature adult—as long as you stick to the chart. And in time, you may be acting like a grown-up simply out of habit. Before you know it, you'll feel ready to be a daddy. Then you'll have the baby, stop getting enough sleep, and completely regress, but you can cross that bridge when you come to it. In the meantime, get to work.

Immature Behavior/
Modified Maturity

Openly and proudly collecting baseball cards/
Buying books in order to accurately assess the current market value of your collection

Buying new clothes to look good for chicks/
Buying new clothes to look good for your superiors at work

Needing time alone to zone out and relax/
Needing time alone to work things out

Buying a car that has great acceleration and sleek lines/
Buying the same car because it has antilock brakes, room in the back, and a good write-up in *Consumer Reports*

Never making the bed because you're just going to get back into it again/
Making the bed because it's an easy way to make her happy

Drinking too much when out with friends/
Drinking too much in the privacy of your own home

Setting up a computer program to keep track of your Rotisserie baseball team/
Setting up a computer program to keep track of your family finances

Playing the stereo too loudly/
Telling the neighbors they're playing their stereo too loudly

Watching the game/
Checking the score

Collecting beer cans/
Recycling beer cans

Being proud of eccentric friends from college/
Being concerned about eccentric friends from college

What You May Be Concerned About
A BUNDLE OF JOY

"How much does having a baby cost?"

If you have to ask, you're grasping at straws. Cost is no reason not to have a baby. A baby can be absolutely free. With home birth, breastfeeding, and gathering nuts and berries, by the time your child is six he will be pulling his own weight. However, the question remains: given a more typical contemporary lifestyle, can you afford a baby?

Item	Cost	What Else You Could Do with the Money	Cost-Saving Tip
Labor and Delivery	$5,000–7,000	Buy a good used car	Consider home birth
Gifts, dining out, flowers to get wife through pregnancy	$3,200	Take an excellent domestic vacation	Compose poems and love letters instead
Pregnancy guide-books; baby name books; Spock in hardcover	$125	Buy Elvis's complete fifties masters *and* Sinatra's Columbia recordings on CD	Borrow from ex-pregnant friends
Clothing (per year)	$750	Buy complete reprint of *Batman* daily comic strips from the 1940s	Wear hand-me-downs
Allowance, ages 0–8	$2,000	Spend wild weekend in Vegas	Practice tough love
Haircuts, ages 0–18	$1,150	Buy a Hi-8 video outfit	Cut hair at home
Education, through grade 12	$80K–200K	Finance a low-budget independent film	Raise a "child actor" to recoup cost
College (4 years)	$250K	4BR, 2BTH, cntrl air, new mechs, patio, grg.	Make kids leave home at 16; get scholarships

CHAPTER TWO
Throughout Your Pregnancy

THE EIGHT DANGER SIGNALS

Most of the little complaints and problems of pregnancy do not require that you turn off the ball game; however, the husband should familiarize himself with the following list of eight dangerous conditions that must be addressed without delay. If they are ignored, serious long-term damage to your relationship is a very real possibility.

Pay attention to your wife at once if you should notice any of the following conditions:

1. *Glamour-Itis.* She is staring down at a magazine and flipping the pages very fast and hard, so that it appears that she isn't actually reading but is most interested in the noise she's making.

2. *Lactose Intolerance.* She serves you a pitcher of milk with your dinner, though you seldom drink the stuff. She may mention or imply that she is tired of drinking six to eight glasses of milk every day. She may also follow up with a few comments: "Something wrong with your milk, dear?" "Why aren't you drinking your milk, dear?" In severe cases she may even pour milk into your beer.

3. *"Fine" Response Syndrome.* She responds to every question or suggestion with "fine," or "sure, fine," or even "fine, that's just fine with me."

4. *Opthalmoduct Flow.* A clear, odorless fluid which seems to leak from her eyes, and is often accompanied by shortness of breath, sobs, and the phrase, "you never understand."

5. *Maternal Reflexism.* She leaves for her mother's without telling you. Call and say you didn't mean it, and *don't* say you have no idea what you've done.

6. *Tourella's Syndrome.* Symptomatically related to Tourette's syndrome, Tourella's is a periodic neurological response that is rarely serious. The typical victim, someone who seldom or never swears (almost always a woman), gets angry enough to attempt an obscenity. These fledgling efforts are ineffective, awkward, and embarrassing for both parties. For example, when trying to call someone (okay, always her husband) a shithead, the typical Tourella victim will instead call him a shitty shit.

7. *Ironic Lyricism.* Her conversational responses tend to be more flowery and poetic than necessary. If you mention you'd like to catch a little boxing on the

tube, she says, "The manly art, ah yes, noble fisticuffs. What was it about 'the sweet science,' my darling? Do tell."

8. *Labor and/or Childbirth*. If your wife is in labor or is actually having a baby (see Chapter Eleven for details), then you should stop ignoring her for a minute and help out. Definitely take off the headphones. Don't guess at what to do, and don't run and boil towels—just do whatever your wife wants.

THE MONTHLY PRENATAL CHECKUPS IN REVIEW

Of course, your wife would love it if you could make it to every appointment, but after you've weighed yourself on the scales and read the magazines, there really isn't that much to do for fun. Anyway, the ob-gyn offices in the hospital are on the same floor as the infertility clinic, so while you may think that you're just being a thoughtful, even doting husband, the other people in the waiting room probably figure you're there to fill a test-tube.

In any case, there are some can't-miss appointments and others that aren't worth the price of admission. Here are our capsule reviews.

The First Visit
Dull, lots of background medical history, information, basic tests. Go if you want to impress the doctor, otherwise . . . pass.

The Second Month
Already repetitive. Wife complains of strange ailments and symptoms. Doctor says it's normal; it's to be expected. Thank you, see you next month, good-bye. A definite . . . pass.

The Third Month
Lovebeat, it's a heartbeat! Now that's entertainment! It may take a few minutes of sliding the walkie-talkie around in the goop on your wife's belly, but when they find that mile-a-minute heartbeat—it's a beautiful thing. So don't miss this one . . . go.

The Fourth Month
More of the same. Your wife keeps trying to come up with something novel to worry about, and the doctor keeps saying it's all perfectly normal, you can't take two aspirin and don't call me in the morning. Unless you think you should be there to prevent your wife from making up symptoms wholesale (feet swelling like balloons, freckle-spread, speaking in tongues) in an effort to have something to worry about . . . pass.

The Fifth Month
Besides the always dramatic weigh-in, there isn't much excitement in the middle months. Unless you feel the need to protect yourself from defamation of character during visits to the doctor in this period, you can just be attentive during the at-home recap, and you can safely . . . pass.

The Sixth Month

Make sure that you don't miss an ultra-sound if your wife is getting one, but otherwise . . . pass.

The Seventh Month

Did you know that on average, the Asiatic elephant's gestation period is over twenty months long? The opossum, on the other hand, is pregnant for about twelve days. Share these interesting facts with your wife, but as for the checkup . . . pass.

The Eighth Month

Still not too much real news, but now is the time for all good men to come to the service of their wives. The final weeks will be a battle, the approaching due date a beacon of hope and fear. It's time to start paying attention, and at the very least, you want to make sure that when you rush into the hospital on the big day, you recognize your obstetrician. Learn her name now . . . . Go.

The Ninth Month

Now the checkups come weekly, but they're also packed with excitement. Is the head down? Can the doctor guess the weight? Does the due date seem right? How early should the baby be taught a second language? As frequently as you can . . . go.

The Six-Week Postpartum

During labor and childbirth you, your wife, the obstetrician, and the nice nurse (not the sullen one) bonded into a devoted, affectionate team. Now it's time for a reunion, when you can show off the gem you all produced . . . . Go.

What You May Be Concerned About
EATING RIGHT

"I've tried to be supportive, and have joined my wife in eating meals that are planned around her special dietary needs during pregnancy. But I'm concerned. Am I doing the right thing?"

Too many perfectly well-intentioned husbands fall into the same trap. What they fail to realize is that a father's special dietary needs are quite different from a pregnant mother's. Your metabolism is different; you are not carrying the child; your needs for iron and minerals are quite different. Simply put, you can eat anything you like. The big question is, will she let you?

For most expectant fathers lunch becomes a key meal. You're at work, away from her watchful eye. The midday meal is often your only chance to depart from the dietary guidelines your pregnant wife is "sharing" with you. The following recommended foods will help you maintain your health throughout your wife's pregnancy. Remember, they are only recommendations—you should feel free to eat whatever you like, whenever you like, whenever you're allowed.

The Raw

Uncooked foods are risky to your wife

BREAKDOWN OF YOUR WIFE'S WEIGHT GAIN

Baby, etc. (placenta, amniotic fliud, uterine enlargement)	12.75 lbs.
Maternal breast tissue	1 lb.
Maternal blood volume, fluids in maternal tissue	5.75 lbs.
Maternal fat (see adjoining column for complete details)	7 lbs.
Total Average Gain	**26.5 lbs**

BREAKDOWN OF YOUR WIFE'S 7-LB. MATERNAL FAT

Milk fats	2.75 lbs.
Eating for two	1.5 lbs.
Häagen Dazs	.75 lbs.
Cream sauces, gravies	.5 lb.
Office birthday cakes it would have been impolite to refuse	.5 lb.
Just-one-bites from husband's desserts	2.5 lbs.
Unfair, inexplicable, punishment-from-God weight gain	1.75 lbs.
Ben & Jerry's	1.5 lbs.
High-salt, high-fat, bagged junk foods too embarrassing to mention by name	1.75 lbs.
Total 7-lb. Gain*	**13.5 lbs.**

*The difference between the seven-pound average gain and the thirteen and a half pounds of maternal fat we calculated cannot be explained. It just kinda snuck up on us.

for all sorts of hard-to-spell medical reasons, so you'll have to keep them to yourself. But that's no reason to miss out on the thrill of eating oddly textured food with the ever-present danger of food poisoning. Go for it!

Sushi
Steak tartare
Rare steak
Any meat bought from street vendors:
    hot dogs, red-hot sausages, souvlaki,
    shish kebab

Junk
Empty calories are dangerous to the well-balanced high-protein, high-calcium diet. But whose diet is that? Not yours. Selections from the empty-calorie food group are the perfect accompaniment to a ball game, working late, or just getting through the midafternoon doldrums.

Potato chips
Pressed potato product in chiplike form
Doughnuts
Popcorn (buttered, see below)
Candy
Cheese puffs

The Greasy
Her intestinal balance is easily disturbed; yours can take it. Prove it to her by eating whatever you damn well please, and plenty of it.

Pizza
French fries

Corn dogs
Grilled cheese
Pastrami

The Spicy
Especially during the period of "morning sickness" but also throughout pregnancy, heavily spiced foods are exclusively the male province.

Biriani
Szechuan
Slim Jims
Mexican

The Stinky
The mere smell of some foods can disturb the pregnant female, so eat 'em at the office and let your co-workers deal.

Thick soups: mulligatawny, minestrone,
    split pea
Stinky cheeses: Gorgonzola, Saga
    blue, etc.
Peanut butter
Wiener schnitzel and sauerkraut

OTHER DIETARY RESTRICTIONS:

Food additives
Fresh fruits and vegetables, simple fish and chicken dishes, locally baked breads, rice, and homemade soup are safe. So when you're on your own? Make sure that you have a plastic wrapper or two to dispose of at the end of every meal.

Alcohol

While discouraged for the mom-to-be, beer is an essential part of any future father's daily intake. It has vitamins B_6 and B_{12}, nutrients that are vital to your immunological system or bone formation or something like that. In any case, we recommend a good cheap local beer. Two or three taken internally each evening will provide a salubrious spiritual cushion.

Caffeine

Not recommended for her, but for you? What better way to jump-start your day? And your body needs caffeine, especially during times of stress and exhaustion. It would be best if you drank a whole lot of coffee, pretty much all day long, but caffeine can also be found in smaller amounts in tea, in some sodas (which also supply large amounts of vital sugar), and in chocolate.

What You May Be Concerned About
WHEN NOT TO CALL THE PRACTITIONER

You should, of course, familiarize yourself with the symptoms and problems of your wife that you should immediately report to your doctor—severe abdominal pain, spotting or bleeding, severe headache, visual disturbances, fainting, dizziness, chills, or fever. However, it is also important to know what symptoms do *not* require immediate attention. By studying these symptoms you can save yourself embarrassing and time-consuming jaunts to the local hospital.

▶ Sudden or severe crankiness

▶ Gradual enlarging of the belly area

▶ Everything going too smoothly

▶ A sudden increase in thirst, swelling or puffiness in the hands, severe headache, fever, fainting, dizziness, sudden weight gain, nausea, or visual disturbances when they occur in the father

▶ Crying during sappy made-for-TV movies, when sad songs are played on the radio, or when there are really cute kids on TV commercials

▶ Generally worried

▶ Need for makeup tips to accentuate "healthy glow"

▶ Sudden worry about the state of public schools in your area.

▶ Your inability to feel the fetal movement even though your wife insists you ought to be able to

▶ Occurrences of any unusual symptoms listed in pregnancy guidebooks in your sister's friend who is pregnant

▶ Constant clumsiness and spilling of drinks

▶ Inability to decide on a name, especially during the first trimester

▶ Her foot has gone to sleep

▶ Inability to find anything good to watch on TV

What You May Be Concerned About
EXERCISE

"We've gotten all sorts of information about exercise for my wife: the Kegel, dromedary droops, and pelvic tilt exercises. What is the right form of exercise for a pregnant father?"

A good rule of thumb is that the easiest exercise is no exercise at all. Occasionally thinking to yourself that you ought to get started on some program but then thinking you don't look *that* bad and realizing that a pretty good hockey game is on TV may not do you any good, but it sure is relaxing.

Still, if you do want to get in shape to help your wife through her pregnancy and to prepare yourself for the rigors of early fatherhood, there are some specific exercises that can help. Remember, you're pregnant too! So start slowly, don't strain, taper off during the last trimester, and avoid contact sports like football, rugby, and kick-boxing.

Wife Catching
Stand in a relaxed position, feet spread slightly, knees bent. Then have an assistant tip a double mattress in your direction. Catch the mattress, then lead it out of the room without breaking any furniture. Repeat, and when you reach a high success level, you'll be well prepared to help your wife maneuver in crowded restaurants in her ninth month.

Labor Coach's Neck Tilt
To prepare yourself for a long and sleepless labor: Sit in a comfortable position. Allow your eyelids to fall slowly over your eyes and tilt your neck to one side; then suddenly jerk your head straight up, open your eyes, and say "Yes, honey?" Repeat fifteen to twenty times daily.

Basic Kegel Exercises
Join your wife when she does her Kegels. Lie on your back with your head supported and your knees up. Let your arms lie flat at your sides. Slowly tense and then relax the muscles in your penis. Do at least twenty-five repetitions. It may not have any particular benefit, but it's a hell of a lot more pleasant than most exercises. And no, you don't have to stretch out first.

Stroll-Ups
Hold a twenty-pound weight under one arm. Stoop down, bending at the knees unless you don't want to, and using your one free hand, change the battery in your watch, stand, and repeat. (This exercise will prepare you for the process of opening or closing a "portable" stroller while holding baby in one arm.)

Running
Sit up suddenly from a comfortable seat. Raise your left arm, pulling your hand outward to reveal your watch. Tilt your head toward your left wrist and say, "Oh shoot, I've gotta run." Get up and leave, making sure your right hand has opened completely and left the beer on the bar.

WHAT NOT TO DO

"She's pregnant, but she won't lie down. My wife is still working, jogging, everything. Isn't a pregnant woman not supposed to lift anything, or do anything?"

Unless her doctor advises otherwise, pregnancy should not prevent your wife from engaging in any of her ordinary activities. Work, sex, even noncontact sports are all basically okay. There are, nonetheless, some strictures. The following activities are to be avoided—as much as possible—as soon as she knows she is pregnant:

Limbo dancing

Bungee cord jumping

Tournament Twister

Rewiring your home using do-it-yourself handbook

Slam dancing

Playing box lacrosse

Asbestos removal

Driving in demolition derbies

Touring sites of nuclear accidents

Sword swallowing

Riding the NASA centrifuge to test G-Force endurance

Bear-baiting

Freedom fighting as a mercenary in Central America

Time travel

QUITTING SMOKING NOW

"I'm trying to quit smoking so my wife and the baby won't have to deal with my secondhand smoke, but I just can't seem to break the habit."

All right. You're eating what you want. You're still knocking off a few brews each evening. Hitting the coffee machine hard. Shouldn't you give up something in the spirit of solidarity? Sure, your father didn't have to quit smoking, but that was then, this is the nineties. It seems like the least you can do, secondhand smoke and all that.

Now, outwrestling the nicotine monkey is never easy, and with the oncoming responsibilities of family—the accelerating financial demands, the endless emotional stress, the constant demands on your time—well, frankly, you deserve to sit back and enjoy some real tobacco satisfaction. BUT YOU CAN'T! Put it out right now. You *can* quit—you can handle it all, and without your skinny little pals.

The key to quitting smoking is to determine what part of smoking appeals to you the most. Is it the nicotine? Or is it oral gratification? Or just something to do with your hands? Think about it. After you decide why smoking appeals to you, just look on the following chart for a simple substitute. After you use the substitute to wean yourself from the noxious weed, then you can work on kicking the substitute. If you can't, just remember: Cigarettes are *not* dangerous for your health. (Until you light them on fire and suck on them.)

APPEALING ASPECT OF SMOKING	SUBSTITUTE
Effects of nicotine	Try the patch, chewing tobacco, snorting snuff
Something to do with my hands	Eat Pixie Stix candy all day long; learn card tricks; grow facial hair and smooth it a lot; scratch privates frequently
Morning headaches	Drink too much, especially warm gin and/or tequila
Enjoy dependency	Take up another addiction: caffeine, gambling, watching television
Carbon monoxide	Inhale automobile fumes, either by taking walks near heavy traffic or in the privacy of your own garage
Yellow staining of hands and mustache	Use food coloring
Dizziness and nausea	Spin in fast circles
"Makes me look cool"	Grow sideburns a little longer; never wear sweaters; get an eye patch

CHAPTER THREE
The First Month

WHAT YOUR WIFE WILL BE COMPLAINING ABOUT

Before She Knows

▶ Exhaustion

▶ You

▶ Not being pregnant after all these months of trying

▶ Her college roommate who gets pregnant every time her husband looks at her

▶ The cost of home pregnancy testing kits

▶ That everyone else in the world seems to be pregnant; "what if we can't get pregnant?"

▶ That you don't believe her when she says she "just feels pregnant"

▶ Nausea

▶ Her voracious sexual appetite

After She Knows

▶ Her complete disinterest in sex

▶ Exhaustion

▶ You

▶ More nausea

▶ Need to urinate frequently, not apparently related to beer drinking

▶ Heartburn and indigestion, flatulence and bloating

▶ Heartburn and indigestion, flatulence and bloating in *you* when you have no right to be complaining

▶ Why last month, or even the month before would have been a better time to get pregnant, because it's miserable being pregnant in the winter (or summer as the case may be)

▶ That the hospital won't let you sign up for Lamaze classes until you're seven months pregnant

▶ Aversions to certain foods—especially chicken soup right after you make a huge vatful

▶ That romantic trip to Paris must happen now—when she feels horrible—or be delayed for a decade or so

▶ Stretch marks (not actual stretch marks, just the concept of stretch marks)

▶ Emotional highs and lows, fear, ecstasy, anxiety, and elation, often all at the same time

A COUPLE OF THINGS TO SAY TO LET HER KNOW YOU'RE CARING, SENSITIVE, AND UP ON THE REQUIRED READING

What your wife is expecting you to read is a whole stack of books, not including this one. To save you the trouble, we have read (all right, skimmed) dozens of books about childbirth and pregnancy and gleaned a few interesting and relevant facts for you to memorize and use. Don't worry about getting caught; if she presses you for details, it's a simple matter to say "Gee, I can't remember exactly where I read that—I've been through so many books now."

Unlike many other sections of this volume, the "Couple of Things to Say . . ." are based on actual, if limited, research, so you can actually *learn* while simply trying to make a good impression.

1. "One early symptom of pregnancy is Montgomery's tubercles, sebaceous glands in the areola of the nipple that become prominent. Shall I check for them?"

2. "Among the battery of tests at your first visit to the ob-gyn will be the Rubella titer that tests for immunity to German measles, so it doesn't matter that you lost your record of childhood immunizations."

3. "Margaret Mead's research in New Guinea found that in some societies boils are considered a typical symptom of pregnancy."

WHAT TO BUY THIS MONTH

Your little bundle of joy will cost you a bundle well before you even get to take it home from the hospital. To help you organize and realistically assess your financial needs in the coming months, we have broken down all the necessary purchases into a set of monthly lists.

If you are superstitious, or just uncomfortable about buying things for the baby before the birth, then don't. There is no reason that you can't buy everything you need the week after the baby has arrived safely (although the credit card company may get panicky and start asking stores to verify your identity).

WHAT YOUR WIFE MAY LOOK LIKE

Throughout the first month her eyes will be agleam, because intuitively she already knows. Her cheeks may be flushed as she probably has a pretty good idea which night it was too. She chooses the clothes she knows you like. Healthy glow? Yes, but alternating with unhealthy greenish glow of morning sickness.

MONTH 1

Estimated Costs, Month One.
Basics: $78
Basics plus extras: $200,078

Basics
Home pregnancy test kit
The real *What to Expect When You're Expecting*
Dr. Spock
A baby name book
Vitamins—for you

Extras
A home in the suburbs
Anything listed in the "What to Buy" section of later months, because you can't wait until you actually *know* that you're pregnant
All the selfish luxury items you won't dare buy as a family man—compact discs, single malt scotch, nice ties, season tickets, monogrammed poker chips

What You May Be Concerned About
SEX DURING PREGNANCY

"Okay, we're not even sure she's pregnant yet, but I'm worried already, so what about sex during pregnancy?"

The approach of fatherhood is a time full of tension, anxiety, and self-doubt. Sex can be the perfect way to relax and escape the pressures. Furthermore, there is no medical or physiological reason to prevent you from engaging in a full sexual life. However, like many men, you may feel uncomfortable about cheating on your wife, so sex is out.

Now might be a good time to take up a diverting hobby like collecting stamps, building plastic models, or watching too much TV. Keep yourself busy and you'll forget all about those troublesome urges, just like the Boy Scout manual said.

What You May Be Concerned About
TIPPLING FOR TWO

"My wife had a few drinks before we knew she was pregnant. Could this be a big problem?"

Probably not. A better indicator of a problem is when the father has *a lot* of drinks *after* he finds out they're pregnant. That's a big problem. As for the young mother, certainly drinking during pregnancy is not recommended, but a few drinks are still statistically very unlikely to cause a problem for the baby. Stop worrying. A generation ago mid-afternoon martinis were standard fare to help pregnant moms relax and unwind. Remember, in France even very young children drink large quantities of wine with every meal, and look at France. On second thought, maybe cutting back a little wouldn't hurt.

What You May Be Concerned About
GENDER PREFERENCE

"I foolishly expressed a slight preference for a boy. Now how do I convince my wife that I won't hate a girl?"

All is not lost. There are two tactics that might work.

The first plan is to say, "I only said that because I thought you had a slight preference for a boy; I would actually much prefer a girl." This lie must then be followed by a full-fledged propaganda campaign: Buy pink booties, talk only about girls' names you like, call the baby "she" at all times, and mention that you heard that girls are much easier to toilet-train, which is true, by the way.

The other plan is to claim that you didn't say it at all; that in fact the cat said it. Be sincerely amazed that the cat talked. Wonder if there's someone you should call. The newspapers? The humane society? The president? Don't budge an inch and eventually your wife may think that you are actually mentally disturbed and under too much pressure. Though not a long-term solution, it may give you enough time for things to cool down.

Judging by these solutions, of course, the best thing is to avoid the situation at all cost. Get your answer down pat now: You want a healthy, happy baby—boy or girl is the furthest thing from your mind. Maintain this attitude without wavering and you'll be all right.

What You May Be Concerned About
TOXOPLASMOSIS

"I've heard that I may be able . . . we may have to get rid of our cats because of the danger of toxoplasmosis."

If you've been dying for an opportunity to get rid of the mangy soulless felines, read your wife the paragraph below: if you actually like cats, skip to the third paragraph.

Cat feces and raw meat often carry the parasitic organism known as *Toxoplasma gondii.* It causes a disease that, although very mild—it often goes unnoticed in those who have its low-grade fever, swollen glands, and rash—poses a serious threat to the fetus of a pregnant woman. It can cause permanent damage, illness, or even death. Cats should be tested but in most cases simply sent away. You should also avoid contact with other people's cats, and avoid gardening in soil that cats may have used as a litter box.

The odds are high that if you have cats or eat raw meat regularly, you long ago contracted the disease and are now immune. A simple test at the doctor's office can establish this for certain. Of the very small number of women who contract the disease, 60 percent don't pass it on to their fetus, and two-thirds of affected babies show no ill effects anyway. Also, damage is unlikely to occur in the first trimester. Just have your cat tested for an active infection, then keep it indoors, away from mice, birds, or other cats. And when pregnant, a woman should let her husband deal with the litter box.

You can dump the cats or keep them. In either case, you should avoid eating any raw or very rare meat. And it almost goes without saying that you certainly shouldn't eat raw cat.

CHAPTER FOUR
The Second Month

WHAT YOUR WIFE WILL BE COMPLAINING ABOUT

▶ Exhaustion

▶ You

▶ Morning sickness

▶ Midmorning sickness

▶ Afternoon sickness

▶ Dusk sickness

▶ Late-evening sickness

▶ Whoever it was who named it morning sickness

▶ The "reassuring" pregnancy books, which terrify her; she can't stop rereading the "What could go wrong" sections

▶ Vitamin supplements, which taste bad—not as good as Flintstones chewables

▶ Also, the size of vitamins, which are "horse pills" so big they are actually filling

▶ That she wants to ask the doctor about terrifying "preeclampsia" but doesn't know how to pronounce it

▶ Sudden realization that child could inherit *your* nose

▶ How she's dying to tell everyone she's pregnant

▶ Occasional headaches, possibly due to hormonal changes, possibly due to your failings as a husband

▶ Milk, which is not a good beverage

▶ Her mother, who has happily informed you that she hasn't thrown out any of her old baby clothes, and that the trunk is in the mail

▶ Fear that cats will be jealous

▶ That too many tearjerker television commercials are about cute kids

▶ That chocolate ice cream is not considered a good source of calcium

▶ Emotional highs and lows, fear, ecstasy, anxiety, and elation, often all at the same time

A COUPLE OF THINGS TO SAY TO LET HER KNOW YOU'RE CARING, SENSITIVE, AND UP ON THE REQUIRED READING

1. "That morning sickness is rough, honey, but at least you don't have *hyperemesis gravidarum*, the rare condition of severe and unremitting vomiting that must be treated with antiemetic drugs. Right?"

2. "Nitrates and nitrites in food can become potentially harmful nitrosamines, so we'll avoid eating cured or commercially prepared hams, bacon, sausage, luncheon meats, smoked fish, Chinese salt-dried fish, raw and smoked salmon or shad."

WHAT TO BUY THIS MONTH

It's never too soon to begin indulging in frivolities and all the things you remember from wherever you last saw actual babies in use. If it looks useful, buy it. If it looks cute, buy it. You, my friend, are a dad-to-be—you need these things.

Estimated Costs, Month Two
Basics: $200
Basics plus extras: $350

Basics
Booties
Bicycle babyseat
Bicycling helmet
Busy box, to hang in crib
Crib mobile
Electric bowl (keeps gruel warm)
Jolly Jumper

Onesies: the adorable little one-piece underwear with the snaps in the crotch
Port-a-Play: toys that you suspend over infants for batting practice
Silver spoon
Teething rings
Videotape of Dumbo

Extras
Baby Shaders, to attach to the inside of car windows to protect baby's eyes from the sun
Eton suit or tiny white lace gown depending on what you're expecting
High-contrast black-and-white crib mobile
Mountain stroller: four-by-four stroller with high underbody clearance and independent four-wheel suspension

WHAT YOUR WIFE MAY LOOK LIKE

Toward the end of the second month she will wear, for the last time ever, that great pair of jeans she's had since college. She may think she's showing, since her belly isn't completely flat. Don't argue the point. Healthy glow? None. Complete takeover by the unhealthy greenish glow of morning sickness.

OR WHAT A FRIEND OF YOURS MAY BE CONCERNED ABOUT

"This friend of mine, not me, was wondering if there's any way of knowing if the baby is definitely his. More specifically, is there a way of establishing this without letting his wife know there is any doubt, because as you can imagine, such a doubt could be extremely destructive to a relationship in and of itself, if you know what I mean."

Whew. You're in big trouble. If you can't find out, you'll be racked with doubts and anxieties. If you try to find out—well, right or wrong, if she finds out that you were trying to find out, it's over.

We guess you just have to hope that your suspicions are not correct. Sorry, that's the best we are going to offer. It's certainly possible that there is a blood test or some other kind of test that could be done in conjunction with amniocentesis, but even in the name of research we wouldn't dare start asking questions about it. Get serious. A guy goes around asking those questions, claiming it's research, and before you know it, someone overhears, passes it on, and boom, marriage over. In this territory even hypothetical questions are just too dangerous. Sorry.

What You May Be Concerned About
THE INTERIM NAME

"We're pregnant, this is fabulous. There's nothing my wife and I would rather do than sit around talking about, well, him or her or it. What should we call our fetus? 'It' seems so impersonal."

Within your wife a new life has sprung into potentiality, and for the next nine months you will be obsessed with charting the development of the fetus into a baby, planning and sacrificing as you enter a new life as parents of . . . him, her, or it.

It seems that every couple has their own solution. For some, it is simply a matter of women's intuition. Just ask your wife if she thinks it's a boy or a girl, and then assume she's right. If she doesn't have a guess, don't worry—complete strangers will soon begin taking one look at your wife and telling you "It's a girl because she's carrying low and wide," or "It's a boy because her skin looks so great." So just find a consensus and go with that gender.

If you're afraid of guessing wrong, creating false expectations, or possibly offending your unborn child, you might want to give it a nickname. One couple we know went with Herbie for reasons known only to themselves. Another called their baby-to-be The Peanut based on a pregnancy book's description of the two-month-old fetus. Still another well-organized couple picked a male and a female name and spoke of "him/her"

and "Megan/Daniel." (Actually, she/he was Megan/Daniel until the fourth month when the husband had second thoughts and started calling him/her Megan/Charles, while his wife stuck with Megan/Daniel, and then after amnio results determined that they were carrying a boy, they settled on Michael, but that's probably a whole lot more than you wanted to know. Although perhaps you should also know that when he was born Michael became Jonathan and still is.)

Basically you should feel free to call him/her whatever you like, whatever makes you both comfortable, with the possible exception of cute diminutives of the scientific names. If you do fall into calling your baby-to-be Fetey, or Embry, keep it to yourselves.

What You May Be Concerned About
AVOIDING COUVADE SYNDROME

"I'm terrified that I may contract this Couvade syndrome thing and get morning sickness, retain water, and have nightmares about stretch marks. How can I avoid a sympathetic pregnancy?"

Couvade syndrome is a psychosomatic condition also known as sympathetic pregnancy. Its male victim suffers from all the symptoms of pregnancy. In the most serious cases, his belly will actually swell. In less serious cases he will simply suffer from morning sickness and general crankiness.

Common sense tells us that the best way to avoid a sympathetic pregnancy is to not be too sympathetic. For most men, this comes naturally, but many may need to work on it. At the first signs of morning sickness in yourself, don't panic, but do take positive steps. Explain to your wife what's going on. When she understands that Couvade syndrome is a potential problem, she will laugh with spiteful delight, but later on she will more than likely understand that right now you just need a little time to be cold, distant, and detached. If you can't absent yourself completely, try to ease off from being sympathetic gradually. Stop listening attentively to her complaints; promise to do little errands and forget them; and when she reads sections of pregnancy books to you, comment on the prose style or question her pronunciation of a word.

If your symptoms persist you may even need to play little pranks on her: Tamper with the bathroom scale, set all the clocks in the house back two hours, or replace her shoes with a pair a whole size smaller. There's no end to the fun you can have, and afterwards you'll both share a good laugh.

Couvade syndrome is unfortunate, but until there is a cure, at least it's nice to know that there are positive steps you can take to minimize its effects.

What You May Be Concerned About
STAYING MARRIED

"We both wanted to have this baby, but now that we're pregnant, we just can't seem to get along. She's so moody and unpredictable."

You're not the only person who has to adjust emotionally to having a baby—this period of transition can be hard on your wife too. And don't forget, she's got all the physical discomforts of pregnancy to deal with as well. So be patient, understanding, forgiving, thoughtful. Listen to all her complaints and criticism without being petulant or defensive. Give, give, give. Buy flowers, write poems, stay home from work, just to take care of her. How can you do it? Simple: by matching every thoughtful act with a passive aggressive jab. A long, low whistle when she steps on the scale ("It was just a joke, sweetie") or cooking heavily spiced stews, chili, thick pungent soups—there are a hundred little ways to needle your mate, and after a long day of feeling put-upon, coming up with them will be second nature.

A second option is to take the offensive. Start complaining about your day the minute you hit the front door, don't even pause for breath for ten to fifteen minutes, and then say, "Oh, baby, I'm sorry. Going on and on about my troubles. How are you feeling?" She'll either buy it or slug you.

The final remedy is to provide your

wife with other outlets for griping. Is she talking to her mother often enough? Does she have plenty of other pregnant friends? Do whatever you can to foster these relationships. Whatever it costs in long-distance bills will be well worth it.

What You May Be Concerned About
COLLEGE

"How can I ensure that our baby is accepted by the college of his or her choice?"

By the second month the initial feelings of joy and/or panic will have worn off, and the time comes for reflection. Expecting a child is a wondrous, joyful, and awe-inspiring experience. With conception came a rush of new feelings, among them an overwhelming sense of responsibility. Parents-to-be not only need to tend to their babies' health and well-being but also need to educate them, instill pride in them, and most of all, give them every possible edge on the competition.

Smart parents know that. Smart parents, for example, know *when* to give birth, what times of the year will allow their child to avoid those unfortunate school-year "cusps" which ensure that the child is either the very oldest or very youngest in their class.

If you didn't think of that, it's water under the bridge. But don't let another opportunity pass you by. Preparation

begins in the womb. If you wait until your baby is born to begin the educational process, they'll probably be okay, just a few steps behind the other kids. What to do? Don't let your fetus spend nine months staring at the uterine walls! Here are just a few ideas.

▶ *Womb Tunes.* Play classical music to the fetus, with the possible exception of Wagner. (If you are less interested in your child's depth of knowledge, and more interested in assuring that he is considered cool, you could choose to play Dylan, Lou Reed, Ry Cooder, and blues guitar legends like Albert King and the Reverend Gary Davis. Just don't forget, when that kid turns fourteen, he will *hate* you. It would be most sensible to begin with Gregorian chants and other early music and work chronologically through baroque all the way to the work of modernists like Copland and John Cage. This will give your unborn child a sense of the continuity and development of musical composition.

▶ *Talk to your womb.* Social skills are just as important as cognitive ones. Make small talk. Establish a sense of propriety and decorum. Speak firmly, with conviction, but offer love and support.

▶ *Buy the right toys for the fetus.* The Press 'n' Play Alphabet, for example, is a wonderful learning tool. These hand-carved wood letters can be pushed against Mommy's tummy to allow the baby-to-be to begin recognizing his letters. There are also many instructive motivational tapes, including *Fetus Self-Improvement*, which provides gentle music superimposed on subliminal messages that will make for a better baby: "Don't cry too much," "When it is dark outside, we sleep," and "Let's make toilet training a priority."

What You May Be Concerned About
LUCKY GUESSES

"I walk into the office one morning, and a female co-worker takes one look at me and says, 'Is your wife pregnant?' I was so flabbergasted, there was no point in trying to lie—the truth was obvious."

It is traditional not to tell anyone about a pregnancy until the first trimester is through, but women's intuition waits for no man. You simply weren't prepared. Every pregnant father should be aware that women's intuition is incredibly powerful, and also quite random. It could be your boss, it could be a co-worker, it could be a woman who hardly knows you at all, but at some time—maybe even before you're even sure that your wife is pregnant—they will ask. Be prepared, stay cool, and *lie*. Your wife is depending on you. Think about it: How are you going to explain that after two months of hiding it from all of your nearest and dearest, you went ahead and told a woman who works in accounts receivable?

CHAPTER FIVE
The Third Month

WHAT YOUR WIFE WILL BE COMPLAINING ABOUT

- Exhaustion
- You
- Excessive salivation (medically known as ptyalism, but don't let her try to say it)
- Unsightly blue lines under the skin in all sorts of places
- Her weight
- Complexion
- Nausea
- Indigestion
- Indigestion tablets, which make her nauseated
- That she's still dying to tell everyone she's pregnant, but is now convinced that people have guessed
- That food tastes funny, and not funny "ha ha"
- That nights are not as long as they used to be
- That not knowing the baby's gender makes it impossible to paint and furnish the nursery, or buy clothes, or stock up on the nifty blue pinstripe disposable diapers for boys or the frilly pink disposables for girls
- Morning sickness
- No morning sickness, so something must be wrong
- That no one ever shows reruns of *My Favorite Martian*
- That Heavenly Hash ice cream is not considered an appropriate source of calcium
- That aspirin and acetaminophen are good drugs, such nice, friendly drugs— how could they be bad for your baby?
- That vitamin pills are so large she needs to eat them with a knife and fork
- That *McCall's* and *Parenting* are still not as interesting as *Vogue* and *Elle*
- Or that *McCall's* and *Parenting* now hold her interest more than *Vogue* and *Elle*, and it scares her
- Emotional highs and lows, fear, ecstasy, anxiety, and elation, often all at the same time

A COUPLE OF THINGS TO SAY TO LET HER KNOW YOU'RE CARING, SENSITIVE, AND UP ON THE REQUIRED READING

1. "Isn't it great to know that right now the placenta is beginning to produce its own progesterone, taking over the function of the corpus luteum?"

2. "You know, the danger of Rh sensitization occurs only when an Rh-negative woman is pregnant with an Rh-positive child—and a simple dose of Rh immunoglobulin soon after delivery will prevent the dangerous antibodies from forming. Honey, are you asleep?"

WHAT TO BUY THIS MONTH

You've got a lot of basics in the closet already, so now you can feel free to purchase actual toys, but don't get behind on the necessities. Just buy, buy, buy, and don't look back.

Estimated Costs, Month Three
Basics: $880
Basics plus extras: $2,595

Basics
Baby book
Bathtub seat
Blankey
Blocks
Cheap pillow for crib
Cigars that announce "It's a Boy" or "It's a Girl" (or bubble gum cigars)
Coloring books
Comb for untangling hair
Crib bumper
Crib pad (under sheet)
Duplos (bigger version of Legos), especially that great zoo set
Hair detangler comb
Knee pads for crawling
Musical pulls
Raggedy Ann or Andy
Rubber Ducky
Shampoo eye shield
Video camera

Extras
BB gun
Legos—an investment for the future
Model train
Tinkle Targets—floatable bull's-eyes for teaching little boys to aim (or make your own by sketching appropriate targets on toilet paper)
Video editing system
Wide-angle lens for video camera

WHAT YOUR WIFE MAY LOOK LIKE

At the beginning of the third month the fetus inside your wife is distinctively human, with a large head, small rump, and fully formed toes and fingers. Though your wife can't feel it, the fetus is now active. The fetus is kicking, clenching and unclenching its fists, pressing its lips together, frowning, and making other facial expressions—and so is your wife, as a matter of fact.

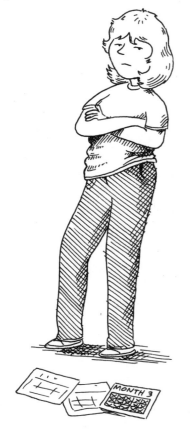

VARICOSE VEINS

"I'll be honest. I think varicose veins are gross. I'd take stretch marks over them any day. Is there anything to do to prevent them?"

To help your wife to avoid varicose veins and other circulation disorders, put two- or three-inch wood blocks under the foot end of your bed. A slightly tilted bed will help balance out the effects of day-long gravity.

An interesting side effect of the tilted bed is adnogginal circulation. All the blood rushes to your head and you may have especially vivid dreams. If you have a severe case, you may have what is known scientifically as "tomato head." If this is the case, you probably have the bed at too steep an angle.

What You May Be Concerned About
BOY OR GIRL?

"Everyone we meet seems to have a very definite idea whether we're having a boy or a girl, based on how my wife is carrying, or her complexion, or the alignment of Jupiter and Mars. Is there any truth to all these old wives' tales?"

Old wives should never be underrated. They're not ultrasound, but then they don't cover your wife's belly with grease and prod her with metal instruments, either. For those who would rather stick with intuition, here are a few of the more popular old wives' tales.

▶ A clear complexion means a girl; a poor complexion means a boy. But girls will cause more headaches during their adolescence, so it all evens out.

▶ Carrying high and long means a boy; low and wide means a girl.

▶ Easy pregnancies are boys; difficult ones girls. No comment.

▶ A dream about trying to pick out a prettier postage stamp means it's a girl; a dream in which you really don't want to stop to ask directions means it's a boy.

▶ Food cravings mean boys; chocolate cravings mean girls.

▶ Italian old wives believe that if you go for the heel of a loaf of bread, it's a boy.

▶ The faster the heartbeat, the more likely it's a girl.

▶ If you put on a lot of weight where you sit, it's a girl.

▶ When the mother gains weight, you're having a baby, but when Dad gains weight? Boy-city.

▶ Pump some stereophonic Motown into the womb. Girls "dance" to music; boys go to sleep. This holds true up to and including junior high school.

▶ Smooth hands mean a girl; rough hands mean a boy; dry scaly hands mean you should be doing the dishes for your wife more often.

▶ Healthy, full-bodied hair? Boy.

▶ If you find yourself getting all your chores around the house done, a boy is on the way. If you're still piddling away the weekend: girl.

▶ Faster-growing leg hair points to a boy.

▶ Whatever the husband thinks, it's the other.

What You May Be Concerned About
HER FOOD CRAVINGS

"My wife still hasn't sent me out to get pickles and ice cream. Is something wrong?"

She will. Some supposedly well researched guides to pregnancy have stated that pickles and ice cream is another old wives' tale. They could not be more wrong. Pickles and ice cream is a simple fact of modern-day pregnancy. Fathers shouldn't feel intimidated or uncomfortable about it. To help expectant fathers serve the very best pickles-and-ice cream combinations to their wives, we offer some suggestions.

As a general rule, the saltier pickles are best with the deeper flavors: the various chocolates—Ultra-Fudge Chunk, Heavenly Hash, Dark Chocolate Thunder—as well as pistachio, coffee, and the cookie crunches.

For the exotics—curry pickles and

sefgurken—we recommend one of the lighter sorbets. To complement the robust flavor of kosher dills, nothing is quite so perfect as peach ice cream. Chowchow pickles, of course, are a natural with chocolate chip. Mint Oreo was positively made to be served up with baby gherkins. Finally, short brine bread-and-butter pickles go best with a simple vanilla.

"We're hip urbanites, and this whole pickles-and-ice-cream concept seems very Iowa. Isn't there something more stylish my wife can crave?"

There is no limit to the foods a pregnant woman can suddenly demand at two A.M. These *nouveaux* cravings can be just as pressing, and twice as difficult to satisfy. Does your twenty-four-hour store carry pasta salad with sun-dried tomatoes? Marinated baby corn? Carrot muffins? Find out *before* you start making foolish promises while you're pulling on your shoes and pants.

What You May Be Concerned About
TELLING

"We've been dying to tell people that we're pregnant, but now that we can, we're not sure how."

The end of the third month, when the danger of miscarriage drops significantly, is the traditional moment to tell the whole world "We're pregnant!" But how? And whom?

Chances are, your wife has already told her best friend and mother. (Do you get to pick a couple of trusted friends? No, *your* friends cannot be trusted.) If you haven't told the grandparents-to-be, they are surely first on your list, and not just because of familial proximity. They should be first because it's good to start with people who will express nothing but total joy and happiness. Unless they are still harboring severe doubts about your chosen mate, or severe misperceptions about their own age, grandkids are the best news there could be.

The rest of the phone calls are up to you. Siblings, close friends, and people with whom you placed bets that you would get pregnant first are priorities. In case you start getting bored with "Guess what?" here are a few ways of giving them the news: We're having a baby; we're expecting; we're in a family way, with child; she's in a delicate condition; preggers, anticipating a blessed event, multiplying, infanticipating, knocked up; or there's a bun in the oven. Most of these will make your wife cringe, even with a bun in her oven, so make the phone calls from another room.

Whom to tell? The basic rule of thumb is that a person should have some sense of who you are before they are informed that you are expecting. But even here, you should decide what is right for you. If it seems important, then by all means let toll collectors, waitresses, and telemarketing representatives in on your joyous news.

One word of warning: The first natural question is "When are you due?" (Unless a more natural question is, "Are you going to get married?" Or possibly, "Are you two out of your minds?") When people ask when you are due, add two weeks to the due date that your doctor estimated and tell everyone—even your nearest and dearest friends and relations—*that* is your due date. Why lie? First of all, the date is nothing but an educated guess. More important, lie because during the final month, especially if you are actually late, you will both be going insane, thanks to people saying "Have you had it yet? " "When was your due date again?" and "Haven't you had that baby yet?" Plus the phone calls from folks "just checking in" accelerate as the due date approaches. When you call home, the first words out of your mouth have to be "No baby! Hi, Mom, it's me, just calling to . . . " Why start all that any earlier than necessary?

CHAPTER SIX
The Fourth Month

WHAT YOUR WIFE WILL BE COMPLAINING ABOUT

▶ Exhaustion

▶ You

▶ That all the other women in the ob-gyn's waiting room are further along

▶ A decrease in urination frequency—a temporary reprieve

▶ That it seems like everyone she meets is pregnant

▶ That her breasts continue to enlarge, and it ain't over till it's over

▶ Leukorrhea (we don't want to talk about it)

▶ Increase in appetite for foods she can't have

▶ Mild edema, a swelling of the feet, ankles, and phone bill

▶ Parents and friends, who were too excited, not excited enough, or just didn't say the right things when she told them

▶ That you told people that she wanted to tell first

▶ That books insist that various strange syndromes are incredibly rare, when she's quite sure she has them

▶ Increased sexual desire or total loss of sexual appetite (no, you don't get to choose)

▶ The size of your home or apartment

▶ Finding herself sitting in the playground for no good reason

▶ That New York Super Fudge Chunk is not considered an appropriate source of calcium

▶ That she just realized there are recessive genes for red hair on both sides of the family and she isn't sure she will be able to bond fully with a red-haired baby

▶ That her regular clothes are uncomfortable, but she's still unwilling to commit to pregnancy clothes

▶ That the NBA playoffs are too long

▶ That books promised, they *promised*, that morning sickness would end, but you don't think her case will hold up in court

▶ Emotional highs and lows, fear, ecstasy, anxiety, and elation, often all at the same time

A COUPLE OF THINGS TO SAY TO LET HER KNOW YOU'RE CARING, SENSITIVE, AND UP ON THE REQUIRED READING

1. "Did you know that right now our baby's sebaceous glands are producing sebum which mixes with skin cells to form the vernix. Vernix! *Our* baby's vernix."

2. "Diuretics to stop water retention—though still prescribed by some doctors—have been shown to be useless and in fact harmful during pregnancy, causing nutritional deficiencies, fatigue, depression, insomnia, and damage to the kidneys. And *Dianetics* is a whole other can of worms."

WHAT TO BUY THIS MONTH

With the passage of the first trimester, the risk of miscarriage is mostly past. Now it is time to forget about the little trinkets and start bringing home the big-ticket items.

Estimated Costs, Month Four
Basics: $1,672
Basics plus extras: $2,082

Basics
Baby-size shoehorn
Barney home videos and licensed apparel
Changing table/dresser
Crayola crayons, in the 64-color box
Crazy straws
Crib
Crib mirror
Food grinder
Glow-in-the-dark stars to stick on nursery ceiling
High chair
High chair cushion
Hip-sling baby carrier
Jug of Desitin
Raffi tapes
Snugli
Spoons shaped like airplanes
Stroller

Extras
Baby Jogger, so baby can have a smooth ride while you take a run; or hang on the garage wall as a nifty device for gathering dust.
Slot car racing set
Saint Bernard dog

WHAT YOUR WIFE MAY LOOK LIKE

The fourth month includes that wonderful moment in between the green morning sickness tones of early pregnancy and the pale, drawn complexion of late pregnancy—yes, the famous "healthy glow." Catch it if you can. Although this is the period when most people make their pregnancy public, your wife will still be dressing in the loose shirts and stretch pants of basic denial wear. She's trying to achieve the "you're hardly showing" look.

Or... she could be of the "dying to show off my pregnancy" school. In that case she may actually develop a swayback accentuating her small rounded belly. She will wear all-out maternity clothes, modeling each outfit for you, pulling the fabric back to ensure that the abdomen is not lost in the folds. (Don't point this out; just say pregnancy becomes her, or she's glowing, or something like that.)

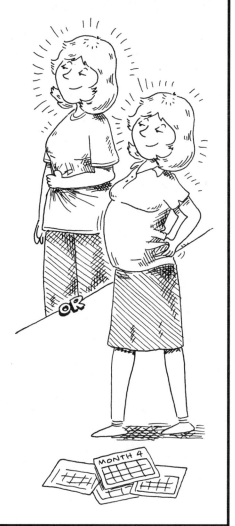

PUBLIC DISPLAYS OF AFFECTION

"Now that my wife is obviously showing, our pregnancy feels so public. I know it's probably ridiculous, but I keep thinking that people will know that we 'did it.' "

Yes, that is ridiculous. Your feelings are silly and wrong. Nonetheless, if you are uncomfortable about this public display of your sexuality, one simple solution would be to tackle the issue head-on. If strangers nod and smile, tell them immediately that you only "did it" once, and it wasn't even that much fun. This will make everyone feel much more comfortable about you and your pregnancy.

Another approach, when you sense public disapproval, is to confront the people and explain quietly, calmly, and in simple but clear language how a man and a woman make a baby. This may not make everyone comfortable, but at least you will all know what happened.

AM I A SEXIST?

"Lately my wife calls me a sexist more and more. I may not be a card-carrying member of NOW, but I was never 'the enemy' before. Is it something about pregnancy that brings out this issue?"

Indeed, pregnancy is a period so obviously unfair to women that it often causes a rising stridency in their responses to gender-related issues. However, avoiding the trap of being dubbed a sexist—and having no defense—is easy if you follow a few simple rules. Stick to the guidelines below and you'll have plenty of ammunition the next time she calls you a soulless troglodyte.

▶ Try to cut down on your use of the expression chickie baby.

▶ Watch a Lifetime made-for-TV movie and pretend to like it.

▶ Use Susan B. Anthony dollars. They're handy once you get used to them.

▶ Even if you mean it as a compliment, never bark at a woman.

▶ Say, "Boy, that Gloria Steinem looks great for her age, doesn't she?"

▶ Watch the NCAA Final Four in women's basketball, too.

▶ Buy some k. d. lang and Suzanne Vega CDs. (For some reason, buying Madonna and Paula Abdul won't help your cause.)

- Stop arguing that figure skating and gymnastics are not really sports.
- Actually read some of the articles in *Glamour* or *New Woman* while you're scanning them for babes.
- The next time something needs to be fixed around the house, offer to bake cookies while she does the repair. And pray she says no.

What You May Be Concerned About
THE RING

"My wife has removed her wedding band. I don't know exactly what she's planning, but I like it here. Should I ask her about it or just wait until I find my stuff outside the front door?"

Relax. Your wife is undoubtedly taking a simple precautionary measure to avoid discomfort when edema (swelling) affects her hands. Shoes, belts, watchbands—everything must be adjusted. In the old days doctors prescribed a low-salt diet to prevent this water retention—but we now know that some salt is necessary. Basically, a pregnant woman's increased blood capacity simply requires a bit of stretching all around. Of course, it is also perfectly normal not to have swelling, so it may well be that your wife has cashed in the jewelry in preparation for the day she hits the road and leaves you crying in your beer. Has she bought a motorcycle lately?

What You May Be Concerned About
FAKING COUVADE

"My wife is now convinced that since I haven't experienced any symptoms of Couvade syndrome—sympathetic pregnancy—that I'm not sympathetic to her plight. Should I fake it?"

You may have to. Once her mind is made up, there will be no point in quoting statistics about the rarity of the syndrome. You'll have to complain about your swollen feet, absentmindedly rub your belly, drink milk, and pretend to throw up every morning. But there are two other approaches you may want to try first.

First, point out to her that psychologically, most Couvade victims are not "sympathetic" but jealous. *Sympathetic pregnancy* is a misnomer and gives too much credit to men who are selfishly trying to co-opt the pregnancy for themselves. You are a well-balanced, sympathetic person—a helpmate and friend—who understands that the burden of pregnancy, along with its joys, will always be the woman's, first and foremost.

If that doesn't work, you may want to try a more general response strategy developed by a team of Northwestern University psychologists led by Dr. Wilma Krobb. They recommend that rather than directly attacking any tender issue, the husband simply make an absurd statement and then defend it vociferously. This is a much more advanced system than Hershimer's, though it is of course based on his ground-breaking treatise, *Changing the Subject.*

Krobb et al. recommend you begin by speculating that the guppies in the fish tank seem to be depressed. The researchers note that the key to success in this strategy is to insist that this is not a casual joke but a terrifying reality. It may seem at first to increase your wife's ire, but if you persist, she will eventually forget what she was talking about. Other possible themes: "A stranger has been in the house," "I suddenly put the pieces together and realized my old college roommate isn't who he says he was," "I keep smelling things from the past."

The worst thing that can happen is that you will actually induce a psychotic episode, and will need professional help to escape the personal demons you have unleashed. Actually, that is pretty bad, isn't it? Well, sometimes drastic measures are called for when you really don't want to start a tiff with the wife.

CHAPTER SEVEN
The Fifth or Sixth Month—Somewhere Around There

WHAT YOUR WIFE WILL STILL BE COMPLAINING ABOUT

▶ Exhaustion

▶ You

▶ Absentmindedness

▶ Fetal movement, not enough or too much

▶ Breast changes: heaviness, fullness, tenderness, tingling, darkening of the areola

▶ Your interest in the above

▶ Absentmindedness. Oh yeah, she already complained about that.

▶ Backaches, side aches, leg aches, fingernail aches

▶ That the eleven o'clock news is too scary

▶ That food cravings are your body's way of telling you what nutrients it needs, so there must be something necessary in chocolate

▶ Mild edema, or a swelling, of the feet, and "mild" is all it takes to make all her shoes, except the ratty slippers, painful to wear

▶ That baby's hiccups have stopped being cute

▶ People stealing the name she wanted to use, and now she can't possibly use it because every other baby has it and the whole point was that she didn't want a trendy name

▶ That you just don't understand

▶ That she has finished reading all the pregnancy books; now needs new sources of anxiety

▶ That cable TV can't run into the bedroom

▶ A recurring need to feel her tummy

▶ That friends and acquaintances need to feel her tummy

▶ That Mint Chocolate Oreo is also not considered an appropriate source of calcium

▶ Emotional highs and lows, fear, ecstasy, anxiety, and elation, often all at the same time.

A COUPLE OF THINGS TO SAY TO LET HER KNOW YOU'RE CARING, SENSITIVE, AND UP ON THE REQUIRED READING

1. "Your complexion looks fine, honey, but if you're worried about it you might want to try a vitamin B_6 supplement of 25 to 50 milligrams—which can help alleviate hormone-related skin blemishes."

2. "Stanislavsky's acting techniques—which involve awareness of the different sets of muscles in the body—can be applied to preparation for childbirth. Perhaps you could have an improvisational birth?"

WHAT TO BUY THIS MONTH, WHATEVER MONTH IT IS

In the rush to buy all the stuff at the toy and baby furniture stores, you've probably overlooked all the little basics you'll need from the local pharmacy. Stock up now, and save on errands later.

Estimated Costs, The Middle Months
Basics: $419
Basics plus extras: $629

Basics
Alphabet and number refrigerator
    magnets
Backpack carrier
Baby bath
Baby lotion
Baby oil
Baby powder
Baby shampoo
Baby toothbrush
Bassinet (no, it's not a musical instrument; ask your wife)
Humidifier
Mechanical swing
Playpen
Portacrib: a travel crib
Walker

Extras
Beatrix Potter, complete 74-volume set
Personalized child-size pool cue
Safety scissors (great for craft projects later; great for your clumsy pregnant wife now)

WHAT YOUR WIFE MAY LOOK LIKE

The belly can be denied no longer and with it comes True Maternity Wear from such haute couture labels as La Stork, Dressing for Two, and Preggers of London. Seemingly overnight facial expression and general complexion have gone from "the joy of pregnancy" to "I've been pregnant forever."

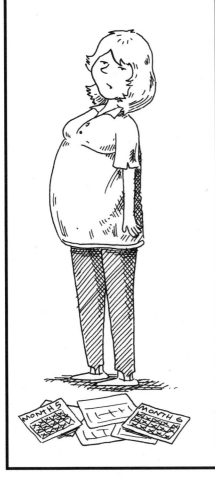

SEX DURING PREGNANCY

"My wife has been, well, sexually hungry just when I'm feeling kind of ambivalent about this odd new body of hers. I've heard this is not unusual, but I don't want to make love that much. Plus, I worry about hurting the baby."

Fear of hurting the baby is a very good "sensitive male" response to your wife's constant sexual demands, but it's far from the only excuse at your disposal. Try: anxiety about burgeoning paternal responsibilities, headache from fine print in pregnancy guidebooks, pulled a muscle constructing the crib, or the "thought we could quit after it worked" argument. If the pressure does not relent, your last, cruel resort is to hint at the unattractiveness of the beached-whale look. Don't take this step without first thinking long and hard about whether you can deal with the repercussions. If you can't figure out the repercussions, you're in deeper trouble than you think. You might want to consider wearing protective headgear at all times.

What You May Be Concerned About
THE DIAPER DEBATE

"I want to use cloth diapers to save the environment, but lately I've heard arguments that disposables aren't that much worse for the world. When we talk to other young parents, we get strong opinions on both sides."

The great diaper debate is one fraught with emotion and righteous indignation. Whichever decision you make, you must be prepared to defend yourself; but have no fear, both sides have plenty of ammunition, and since, deep down, you've already made your decision, just pick a list and prepare to argue.

IF YOU HAVE MORE OR LESS DECIDED YOU CAN'T PASS UP ON THE SHEER CONVENIENCE OF DISPOSABLES, READ THIS LIST

▶ The latest research by garbologists shows that disposable diapers are actually no worse for the environment than cloth diapers.

▶ You use far fewer of them because their absorbency level is one of the true modern miracles of science. You can leave your kid in one for about a week.

▶ The processing cost of sanitizing all those cloth diapers—in energy, clean water, and air and water pollution—is staggering.

▶ Hundreds of diaper service delivery trucks spew unnecessary carbon monoxide into the air.

▶ You have to buy disposables for travel anyway, and you travel a lot.

▶ There is no diaper service available in your area, and washing them yourself is icky.

▶ Disposable diapers take up less than 1 percent of landfills—newspapers use up a much higher percentage, so if we could just all learn to recycle newspapers, then we could afford to use disposables.

IF YOU HAVE MORE OR LESS DECIDED THAT SAVING THE WORLD DEPENDS ON YOUR CHOICE OF CLOTH DIAPERS, READ THIS LIST

▶ Cloth is obviously the more ecologically sound choice. When people argue for disposable, they are grasping at straws, out of self-indulgence.

▶ Cloth diapers can be used many times, then reused as dust rags, and finally recycled into other materials.

▶ Cotton biodegrades easily.

▶ The exhaust fumes from the delivery trucks? Are you planning to go pick up disposables at the store in your horse-and-buggy? Sure, you'll get them with the other groceries sometimes, but believe us, you'll make a few trips just for diapers.

▶ The industrial pollution caused by creating and cleaning cloth diapers is probably much milder than the industrial pollution caused in the more complicated manufacture of disposables.

▶ Plastic never goes away.

▶ You know what makes those disposables such miracles of absorbency? Chemicals! Weird man-made chemicals about which little is known. Do you want more of these in the world? Do you want these soaking against your baby's skin? Cotton is all natural; cotton has been worn for hundreds of years.

What You May Be Concerned About
BECOMING A FATHER

"Just being pregnant has meant so many changes in our lifestyle, our planning, our relationship. The prospect of fatherhood is beginning to terrify me."

Having a child will mean changes, no doubt about it. Along with the great joy and satisfaction that the baby will bring into your home come limitations, sacrifices, worries. You should prepare by tapering off. Adjusting now to just a few of the deprivations to come will make the initial shock of fatherhood that much easier. Here are ten simple ways to get ready.

1. Stop seeing movies in the theater. Young parents only see movies on video, so if you don't stop going out to the movies now, there will be an awkward "lag" of six to eight months during which every new video release is a movie you've already seen.

2. Explore take-out options. You'll want more choices than pizza and Chinese when you're eating it every night of the week.

3. Check out the late-night television schedule: Dobie Gillis, Joe Franklin, and Larry King will help you walk baby to sleep. If you start watching now, you may get hooked and actually look forward to those two A.M. feedings.

4. If your wife can't get to sleep, drive her around the block seventeen times and then carry her back into the house.

5. Go to the drugstore and say loudly, and without shame, "Excuse me, where are the wipes?" Might as well buy a few now.

6. If you smoke, try doing it secretly in the garage. Do it barefoot too. The cold cement adds to the effect. Don't put it out with your foot, though, and don't forget to pick up the butts *and* the spent matches.

7. Slice a hot dog into ten sections, then cut each circle into choke-proof quarters, and allow to cool and dry out for one hour. Finally, eat the whole thing yourself because the kid wasn't interested. Use a spoon, in case you hadn't figured that out.

8. Practice holding your breath for two minutes and seventeen seconds. (The amount of time a skilled parent takes to handle a particularly foul diaper change.)

9. Buy yourself clothes that are too small, then pack them in boxes, carefully label them, store them, and forget about them forever. It may seem pointless, but so are

bathrobes for one-year-olds, and we own two.

10. Carry a ten-pound sack of sugar everywhere you go to build upper-body strength.

What You May Be Concerned About
TAKING THE PLEDGE

"I'm trying to support my wife by joining her in giving up smoking, drinking, and coffee, but it's driving me crazy."

It's great to be supportive, and it is almost guaranteed that your wife will find your temperance admirable. She will feel that you are working as a team, and also she won't have to face temptation from your cigarettes, martinis, or French Roast. If you can do it, Godspeed, Oh Perfect Husband!

We recommend another approach. Since she can't drink or smoke and may be cutting back on caffeine, you should think of yourself as smoking for two and drinking for two. If your wife can eat for the baby and for herself, surely you can order a double and drink a toast to your better half!

And by the way, here's the good news: The day your wife found out she was pregnant, she became your designated driver for the next year. It's a handy thing, too, because you could use a drink.

PREGNANCY AND CHILDBIRTH IN TV-LAND

What is the father's role in pregnancy? The answer leaps to mind: to pace back and forth in a waiting room, looking exhausted, then be joyful and flustered with the news, and finally be well-meaning but incompetent at handling the baby. Where does this ideal of fatherhood come from? TV-Land, the place where life sure is complicated, but nobody really gets hurt.

To better understand our own perceptions about childbirth and pregnancy, we must understand where those perceptions came from. The answer, for better or worse, is television. Only by examining the "myths" and ideals of fatherhood from the small screen can we begin to understand ourselves.

Career Woman
When 99 and Max finally tied the knot —even before the twins were born— she gave up her career for him: "I found that there just weren't enough hours in the day to be an efficient housewife and a good spy."

Career Woman, Part II
Lucille Ball surely pulled off the ultimate juggle of career and family when, on January 19, 1953, she gave birth both on-screen and off. Little Ricky was born on *I Love Lucy* on the same day that Lucille Ball, via cesarean, gave birth to

Desi Arnaz, Jr. The cover of *TV Guide* and huge ratings resulted.

Cigar-Passing

When Ted Baxter finally gave birth—with Georgette's help—the normally ungenerous newscaster from *The Mary Tyler Moore Show* was effusive: "I'm a daddy, I'm a daddy—have a cigarette."

Diapers

When *All in the Family's* Archie Bunker had grandson Joey, the network censors did not want him to be seen changing Joey's diapers. The show resisted and shot the scenes—from discreet angles of course—and American television had a new first.

Drinking During Pregnancy

Worried about drinking during your pregnancy? It is best to avoid drinking, but remember that our mothers drank and smoked all pregnancy long, and it may not have been good for us, but we survived. There is an episode of *Bewitched* that underscores the attitudes of an earlier era. Mrs. Tate (Darrin's boss's wife) is anxious about telling her husband Larry that she just found out that she is pregnant. Samantha helps her overcome her anxieties by giving her a pep talk and by pouring her numerous martinis. Of course, due to an overheard conversation, Larry and Darrin arrive under the mistaken impression that Samantha is the one who is pregnant and keeping it a secret. The episode is rarely shown in syndication because of the martinis.

Driving

The main focus of many pregnant fathers in TV-Land is the drive to the hospital. Their responsibility begins with the first pangs of labor and ends when their wife is safely delivered to the hospital. After that it's all pacing. Rob Petrie on *The Dick Van Dyke Show* lay in bed fully dressed, and in a famous bit, practiced leaping up and putting on his hat in one quick motion to slice a few tenths of a second off that all-important car trip. When 99 was expecting the twins, Maxwell Smart spent most of his time figuring out the fastest possible route to the hospital. Of course, when the time finally came, he accidentally drove right into a Kaos trap — part of an exciting two-parter called "And Baby Makes Four."

Eggs

Mork—as Orkan males will—gave birth to the egg out of which "Mirth" (Jonathan Winters) emerged. The less you think about this the better.

Fear of Fatherhood

Another episode of *Bewitched* approaches—metaphorically—our fear of fatherhood. Spurred on by Samantha's pregnancy Darrin dreams of offspring that inherit her magic powers and taunt him by flying in circles around his outstretched arms. Our own fears may be more pedestrian—but all fathers must eventually deal with the fear that their children will surpass them.

Pain Relief

Did Samantha Stevens consider using magic to spare herself the pain of labor and childbirth? The *Bewitched* episodes surrounding the birth of Tabitha and later Adam are unclear, but judging from her chipper look in the hospital, you can bet she isn't worried about her episiotomy stitches.

Where Babies Come From

In the early years of television, birth was discussed only in veiled terms. The word "pregnant," for example, was forbidden. As you can imagine, there weren't a lot of jokes about women rupturing their amniotic fluid in the grocery store. The addition of children to a family was almost always non-biological in nature.

When Jeff and Mary Stone started getting long in the tooth, for example, Donna Reed added to her brood by adopting Tris—a little girl who follows them home from the park one day. Try explaining that in terms of birds and bees.

My Three Sons explored both adoption and natural additions. Ernie was adopted when Mike moved out. But Robbie and Katie eventually had the triplets—Steve Jr., Charley, and Robbie II—while Steve, the patriarch, went back to adoption by marrying Dodie's mother Barbara.

A Final Note

As you re-examine television, your wife may doubt that your motives are pure. She may feel that watching so much TV is a waste of time. One way to combat her criticism is to enlist her as a fellow viewer. Tell her, and this is quite true, that in certain segments of the market research done by the Nielsen Ratings, a pregnant woman is statistically considered to be two viewers. It may seem strange, but for marketers of baby and child care products—diapers, toys, rug cleaners—this is a valid measurement of the impact their television commercials are having, so your wife is, quantitatively speaking, watching for two.

CHAPTER EIGHT
The Seventh Month

WHAT YOUR WIFE WILL CONSTANTLY BE COMPLAINING ABOUT

▶ Exhaustion

▶ You

▶ Clumsiness, disorientation, headache—basically it's like being drunk without having any fun

▶ Shortness of breath, dizziness, heartburn, nasal congestion—or it's like smoking without getting to light up

▶ Strong and frequent fetal movement—and the novelty has worn off

▶ That she's tired of complaining about same old symptoms and wants new symptoms

▶ Itchy abdomen

▶ High cost (and limited use) of maternity panty hose

▶ That she always gets called on to demonstrate in Lamaze class

▶ Sciatic nerve problems, which are both painful and difficult to pronounce

▶ Her company's maternity leave policy

▶ That your company has never even heard of paternity leave

▶ That her best friend's ob-gyn sounds nicer than hers

▶ Her weight

▶ That ultrasound pictures are too impressionistic

▶ That people make jokes when she enters elevators

▶ That medical textbooks (for complete, scientific details of every single possible problem) are expensive and their prose style is tedious

▶ Nonalcoholic beer, which just doesn't do it

▶ Just realized that baby won't arrive in time to be a deduction for the current tax year

▶ ESPN

▶ That she doesn't want to know what sex the baby is, but it seems unfair that the doctors know

▶ That you haven't read any of the pregnancy books

▶ Emotional highs and lows, fear, ecstasy, anxiety, and elation, often all at the same time

A COUPLE OF THINGS TO SAY TO LET HER KNOW YOU'RE CARING, SENSITIVE, AND UP ON THE REQUIRED READING

1. "You know they say that vitamin E can be very helpful in preventing varicose veins; of course, I mean vitamin E in the form of d-alpha tocopherol acetate. Mixed tocopherols don't have any effect on varicose veins, naturally."

2. "You can practice the breathing techniques you learn in class by trying to control the pain of a headache, or a stubbed toe. Every little accident is an opportunity."

WHAT TO BUY THIS MONTH

By now many pregnant couples will know their baby's gender and so can begin reinforcing sexual stereotypes by choosing boy or girl clothes, boy or girl colors for the nursery, and boy or girl careers for which to press.

Estimated Costs, Month Seven
Basics: $722
Basics plus extras: $2,490, plus $14.95 per month

Basics
Audiotape lullabies
Baby monitors
Baby sweater with fruit motif; or baby sweater with truck motif
Bathtub (infant-size, not regular)
Child-size bathroom sink (fits in tub)
Infant-size party dress or baseball uniform

Juice dispenser
Nightlight
Nursery art
Piggy bank
Rocking chair
Supply of disposable diapers; the blue pinstripe or pink flowers
Teeny-tiny baby fingernail clippers
Travel diaper kit

Extras
Cable TV premium channels (parents really never go out)
Christening gown (if you're christening)
Dr. Seuss, complete (don't forget his books published under the pseudonyms Rosetta Stone, Theo LeSieg, etc.)
Tiara or football helmet
Second VCR (see "Cable TV" above)

WHAT YOUR WIFE MAY LOOK LIKE

That healthy white glow is now here to stay, and she is too tired to make any sort of facial expression at all. Yes, her breasts are now larger. No, you can't touch them—they're painfully sensitive. She will also stop denying the need to get off her feet, to the point of asking old ladies and war veterans to give up their seats for her.

LET'S BE ALARMIST

"Reassurance, reassurance, reassurance. My wife and I are sick of all the books and doctors and friends comforting us and telling us that there's nothing much to worry about. We want to worry."

Most people would like to go through all nine months of pregnancy thinking happy thoughts, but let's face it, you're not really pregnant if you're not going crazy worrying about all the things that could go wrong, feeling guilty about all the little things you may have done wrong, and poring over every new pregnancy and childbirth article in the newspapers and magazines. Paranoia is a perfectly healthy reaction to pregnancy.

We have already promised that this book would not raise unreasonable fears, so we feel honor-bound not to tell you that your tap water may already be limiting your child's intellectual potential; nor will we tell you which brands of coffee use seeds sprayed with dangerous pesticides. It would also be wrong for us even to bring up such unlikely disorders as Flander's syndrome, fetopelvic melanoma, or even gestational aneuristic halitosis. Their incidence is so statistically improbable that they are hardly worth mentioning. There are, however, many other books that can fill you in on all the details. Go to the store, buy them all, pore over them constantly, and do it before it's too late. If you still find that your need for anxiety is outstripping the available literature on pregnancy, you might want to start in on reading books about the sorry state of America's educational system, the effect of television of modern culture, or the fragility of the ecosphere.

What You May Be Concerned About
SEX DURING PREGNANCY

"What exactly are the chances of having sex during pregnancy?"

Sexual relations during this physically and emotionally traumatic period are nothing to worry about. You should remember that the statistical chances of having sex during pregnancy are very low, almost negligible. Odds are you'll never have to deal with it. Still, every pregnant father worries about it, and yes, it could happen to you. If your wife is feeling amorous, don't panic. Yes, she can be an intimidating physical presence, but if you proceed with caution, and don't bring any unrealistic expectation to the process, you may find that you actually enjoy it.

What You May Be Concerned About
DOING THE LAMAZE

"Do I really have to take classes in childbirth? Can't I just read a pamphlet for a few tips and just be really pleasant and positive during labor?"

Don't let the prospect of a few tedious classes keep you from Lamaze (or whatever method your hospital offers). This is your one chance to do something useful! You're the coach, man, and whether your personal style is more Vince Lombardi or Pat Riley, this is an opportunity to get involved.

Use the classes to get yourself into a child-birthin' frame of mind. The game is tied and going into the ninth inning. It's overtime, gut-check time, and you had better know what all your options are. What will you do if the obstetrician notices a breech condition and calls an audible for a cesarean? What if your wife is clearly tiring, but the anesthesiologist says it's too late for an epidural? If you're going to coach this birth, you better have a game plan and Lamaze is the place to get it.

The classes themselves vary greatly from instructor to instructor. The better instructors show a lot of films, go over breathing and relaxation techniques every week, talk a lot about pain, and otherwise provide down-and-dirty preparation. The worst classes start at the very beginning, like a sort of remedial health class. You'll get the charts of the fallopian tubes, the egg and the sperm, even mitosis and meiosis if you're really unlucky. Then they walk you through fetal development, and only get to the breathing gimmicks and "Choices in Pain Relief" in the last meeting or two. The only advantage of this type of class is that they are slightly more likely to give you a small suitable-for-framing diploma in childbirth.

What You May Be Concerned About
HOME ALONE

"My wife is considering a home birth. But I don't know, I guess I'm more traditional."

What are you talking about? You're not more traditional, you're more sane. Home birth?! Yeesh! All right, pregnancy isn't a disease, and modern hospital care may be a little dehumanizing and expensive, and skyrocketing malpractice awards make doctors too quick to go to a C-section. Sure, sure, sure, but those are not reasons to just give up and stay home. What if the phone rings right in the middle of active labor? Anyway, does your bed at home adjust to seventy-five different positions? Is your television mounted to the ceiling? Go to the hospital, you'll love it. In fact, more often than not, your wife won't want to leave the twenty-four-hour nurse attendants, the comfortable adjustable bed with handy swivel tray, and the free babysitting. Only the food will urge her out and on her way.

What You May Be Concerned About
PREGNANCY SIMULATIONS

"My wife says I'm a jerk. While that seems to me to be a rather broad, overgeneralized statement, she has suggested that I go to one of these pregnancy-simulation weekends. What are they like?"

It may not be the cure for jerkiness, but a well-managed, professionally run pregnancy simulation weekend can change your attitude about what your wife is going through. The specifics vary, but basically these camps and spas attempt to approximate the experience of late pregnancy. Naturally, it begins when you strap on a forty- to seventy-pound water-filled "womb." (Your womb is heavier than your wife's because it is in proportion to your body weight—no breaks, mister.) You then ingest some mild drugs, which will make you feel disoriented, experience strange dreams, experience mood swings, and want to pee every half hour. While the staff smoke and drink in front of you, you'll enjoy a smorgasbord of fresh vegetables, whole wheat, bran, iron- and calcium-rich foods, and of course, pitchers of milk. For further details, just call or write.

The Nine-Month Weekend
    Mount Kisco, New York. (National headquarters, other locations available.)

What You May be Concerned About
RUBBER BABY BUGGY BUMPERS

"Some acquaintances seem to think that the wife's belly is fair game — they rub without even asking!"

As the due date approaches you will find that—much like rubbing the Buddha's belly—it seems to be considered good luck to feel that taut kettle drum that your wife is lugging around. The standard etiquette books offer little advice when it comes to patting other people's bellies. Is it acceptable among relatives? Close friends? Female acquaintances only? In a business setting? While pregnant women will have varying tolerance for the intrusion, most observers agree that by the eighth month, all pregnant bellies are awfully tempting targets.

The one group of would-be belly rubber that must be turned down definitively are the ones who ask you, not her, for permission, as though you are the proprietor of a traveling freak show. It may seem difficult to turn down a polite request, but it really isn't. No explanation, or diplomacy is necessary. All you need to do is feign complete horror at the suggestion. Furrow your brow and let your mouth drop open, as though they had asked permission to feel your armpit.

If, on the other hand, your wife is *not* shy about sharing her overgrown personal space, and positively wants people to feel the baby kicking, then you might as well charge a couple of bucks. You can probably bump it to five or ten when the baby is kicking. It may seem mercenary, but formula ain't free.

CHAPTER NINE
The Eighth Month

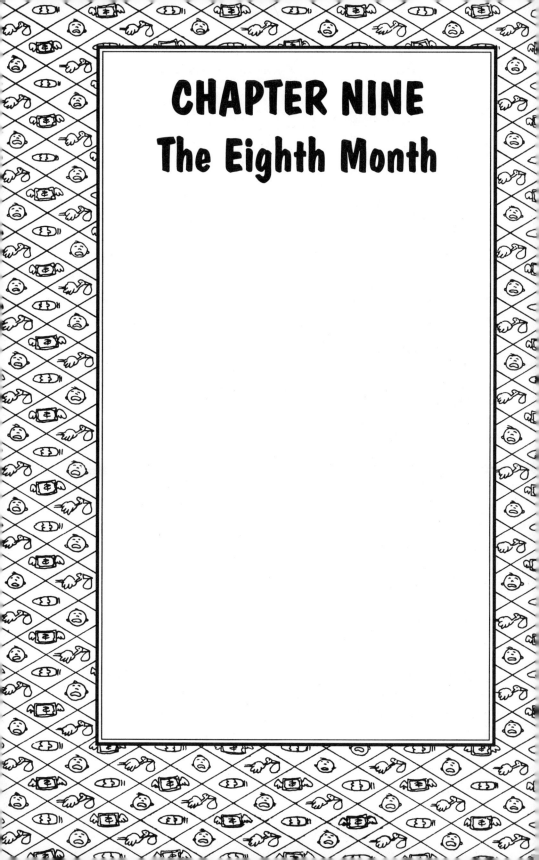

WHAT YOUR WIFE WILL BE COMPLAINING ABOUT

▶ Exhaustion

▶ You

▶ How much room you take up in the bed

▶ Her weight

▶ Bleeding gums

▶ That low-sodium food is low-tasty

▶ Unattractive distortion of her bellybutton

▶ Strong, uncomfortable fetal movement (new nickname for Fetus: The Karate Kid)

▶ The distance between the TV and the bathroom

▶ Braxton Hicks contractions—if that was one, she doesn't want anything to do with real contractions

▶ That a month is a very long time

▶ That you never raise your hand in Lamaze class

▶ Waistbands of maternity pants—do they go over the belly or under it?

▶ Extremely vivid and terrifying dreams

▶ That foreign teams always win the Little League world series

▶ That no guarantees are available for due dates

▶ That you just don't understand

▶ Hanna Andersson and Biobottoms catalogs, which are full of cute but too-expensive stuff

▶ Pregnancy vitamin pills—too large to swallow but too small to balance a cup of tea on

▶ That she really misses sushi

▶ Nicknames you have given her lately (Moby, Barge, Dromedary, Her Hugeness)

▶ Disorientation and inability to focus—she now consistently loses to you at Scrabble

▶ That even Cherry Garcia is not considered an appropriate source of calcium

▶ Emotional highs and lows, fear, ecstasy, anxiety, and elation, often all at the same time

A COUPLE OF THINGS TO SAY TO LET HER KNOW YOU'RE CARING, SENSITIVE, AND UP ON THE REQUIRED READING

Remember, unlike much of the information in this book, these are actual facts discovered in the actual reading of other books.

1. "Fetoscopy—which is less common than ultrasound or amniocentesis—allows doctors to photograph the fetus. But it is still primarily experimental, so we don't have to worry about it."

2. "When the baby has the hiccups, it may be because he is actually practicing breathing in the amniotic fluid."

3. "The breathing techniques from childbirth class are found in other cultures. The Zulu, for example, teach pregnant women to go to the door of their hut each morning and breathe through each nostril, alternately."

WHAT TO BUY THIS MONTH

Don't panic! So you're out of money—you can't be out of credit yet. And if you are, start hitting up the folks. After all, they wanted this child as much as anyone.

Estimated Costs, Month Eight
Basics: $275
Basics plus extras: $410

Basics
Baby thermometer
Baseball glove
Diaper pail
Frozen dinners
Hooded baby towel
Ipecac syrup
Juice canteen
Nasal aspirator
Stuffed Teddy bear
Swaddling
Supply of baby Tylenol
Velcro diaper covers
Washclothes

Extras
Catcher's mitt/first baseman's glove
Clothing with team logos
Clothing with the insignia of the university you expect your child to strive to get into (especially bibs)
Clothing with family crest
Wipe warmer, which electronically warms diaper wipes for easy changes (some models also warm shaving cream)

WHAT YOUR WIFE MAY LOOK LIKE

The eighth month is when the slight waddle appears, especially toward the end of the month. By now she will have gained twenty-five to forty-five pounds and yet look, with her drawn face, like she is starving. Most of her fashion choices are now made on the basis of how easy they are to deal with when she needs to pee every twenty minutes.

SEX DURING PREGNANCY

"My wife is so big, but she's so happy not to be using birth control that we're having more sex than ever. Are there any limitations we should be aware of in late pregnancy?"

Good for you. Next time write to *Penthouse*, maybe they'll care. Okay, fine, what was the question again? Oh, yes, limitations. As far as strictures go, basically, unless your doctor indicates otherwise, a healthy pregnancy should cause no limitations so long as you are both comfortable, with the only exception being that it is important not to blow air into your wife's vagina during oral sex. If this limitation creates a major problem for you, then you know something we don't.

FETAL ANGER

"My wife has had a lot of discomfort with the baby kicking up a storm. In fact, I'm trying to convince her that he doesn't have a grudge against her. That isn't possible, is it?"

Fetal distress is one thing; fetal emotional distress is another. The first is a physiological problem; the second is a psychological problem—in the mother. Unless you're a strong believer in original sin, or suffer from extreme paranoia (which is not unusual at this stage of pregnancy), it is reasonable to assume the baby holds no grudges. She's not mad at her mother, she's just getting crowded, feeling pressured, and finally kicking back. The same basic process will happen during adolescence.

What You May Be Concerned About
THE BABY BOOK

"We want to make a nice baby book, but everything we've seen is just too adorable for words. What should we do?"

It is handy to have a book that lays it all out for you—from "Your impressions of baby's first moments," "First birthday party," "First words," all the way to "Baby's first act of crummy teenage rebellion." But such books limit your creativity. Why not make your own? It's the politically correct thing to do! You should decide for yourself what's important, and in any case, you probably won't get beyond about the second month before the book just becomes a convenient holder for keepsakes that you're going to glue in and annotate "one of these days." (Why not just keep a few stray notes and wait until the kid is old enough to put it together without your help. It's their book, after all.)

You can think of all the basic keepsakes, significant moments, and plenty more, but here are a few suggestions to get you started.

▶ ID bracelet from hospital (have you checked it, by the way?)

▶ Pressed flower from bouquet sent to Mom

▶ Pressed belly-button stump

▶ Hospital bill (start in on the guilt from day one)

▶ Newspaper clippings from the day Baby was born: headlines, baseball standings, movie listings, horoscope, weather report, lottery numbers, real estate listings, and oh that "Marmaduke"

▶ First time Baby was dropped on head and screamed so much it scared the hell out of you

▶ First bad haircut

▶ First time Baby reached over and hung up important long-distance phone call

▶ First time Baby allowed a hat to stay on for more than two seconds

▶ First time Baby found television sitcoms predictable (look for this one, generally, at around age eight to nine months)

▶ Souvenir shard from the first piece of antique crystal Baby destroys

▶ First time a hypnotist convinced Baby to act like a chicken

THE LEAST COMPLETE BABY NAME GUIDE

Michael for a boy, and Diane for a girl. There, done. You don't even have to read the rest of this section.

Not good enough, huh? Well, it is true that naming your child is an extremely personal, idiosyncratic process. No two couples go about it the same way. Actually there were two couples that went about it the same way, but it turned out that each father treasured a broken gold medallion, each was adopted, each married a woman named Helen, and each believed that Steely Dan was an underrated band, but that's another story and a very long one too. You just want to name your baby.

Naming the baby is a joyful and creative task, but it can be a sincerely awe-inspiring task too. Naming implies possession, total responsibility. It is the first time that you must see your baby not as a mere miracle of nature, but as a future participant in society. A name gives a child reality, definition, future. The implications are enormous. Names can be traditional—and stereotypical. They can be poetic—and strange. They can bespeak glamour or simplicity, strength or wisdom, multiculturalism or rabid fundamentalism—all in a tiny being who has got a few reflexes, a gnarly fresh bellybutton and 20-400 vision. And you thought naming your cat was hard. What are you going to do?

Play it safe and stick to our list. Sure, no one will tell you, "Oh that's a beautiful name!" but that's okay because when they do say that, what they're really thinking is, "Why do bad names happen to cute babies?" Here are five good names for each sex that may be a little dull, but that's what names should be: safe and innocuous.

Don't waste your cash on some 50,000-name paperback—this is plenty to choose from.

BOYS: Charles, Michael, Daniel, William, Brian

GIRLS: Elizabeth, Michelle, Jane, Susan, Alexandra

A Baby-Namer's Bonus Tip: no matter how thankful you are, don't name the baby Epidural, or even Epi. If you really feel the need to thank the pain reliever, perhaps the name of your anesthesiologist would be a better choice. Best of all, wait a few days. You may find that your extreme appreciation will pass.

WHAT TO NAME YOUR BABY WHEN YOU'RE NOT SERIOUS ABOUT NAMING YOUR BABY

It has now been established through genetic-mapping that one of the traits linked to the male sex is obsessive joking when faced with the task of naming a baby. Even before the physiological research, field observation had clearly supported the theory. According to 1990 figures, the average pregnant woman finds 3.5 joke names amusing, and will laugh politely at roughly 7.7 names; a pregnant father, however, will laugh at up to 78.5 ridiculous names that he himself has made up. The disparity is a problem. However, the solution is simple. Men should simply realize that joking about names is to be saved for office and poker-night banter. Women should understand that the urge to make stupid suggestions is almost irresistible. For example, the list below has no real practical purpose except that, as a typical man, the author couldn't resist.

Boys	Girls
Blind Lemon	Bertrude
Dagbert	Duchess
Enos	Eccentricia
Fonz	February
Fudgie	Jersey
George Foreman VI	Kermette
Itchy	Mercedes
Laddie	Moxie
Pogo	Mylar
The Truth	Petunia
Upchuck	Pip
Walmart	Spaldeen
Zebulon	Taffeta

What You May Be Concerned About
IT'S JUST A DREAM

"Lately my wife's dreams have become especially vivid. But when she tells them to me, I am still incredibly bored. Is there something wrong with me?"

Not at all. During the last trimester a woman's dreams become wilder and will seem frighteningly real to her. Natural anxieties, hormonal changes, and sleep deprivation account for this, but there is nothing more tedious than hearing a dream. "Say, that reminds me of a story that has no particular beginning or end and doesn't make any sense. Care to hear it?" Oh, sure honey, just let me know when a character is no longer who they started out as, or when you completely change where you are, okay?

And if you're thinking that you could try to interpret her dreams symbolically, forget it. First, the chances are good that your effort will make her cry. Second, these dreams are so bizarre that they defy conventional interpretation. Experienced Freudian analysts have been known to hear the dreams of women in the third trimester and say nothing but "Whoa, that's weird!"

If she or you would still like to have a go at interpretation, use the basic guide on the following page.

WHAT TO DREAM WHEN YOU'RE DREAMING

The dreams of pregnant women—spurred on by hormonal shift, increased blood circulation, and natural anxieties—become incredibly vivid, sometimes frighteningly so. It can be reassuring to understand where these dreams come from, and who better than the husband to play psychologist?

As you do your analysis, realize that dreams cannot be understood merely as a group of symbols with standardized interpretations. The imagery of dreams has specific, personal meanings that defy simple attempts to classify and demarcate. On the other hand, dreams cannot be understood much at all, so you might as well try our glossary.

Here is your basic dictionary of dream symbols specific to pregnancy. Remember, our interpretations apply only to your wife's dreams. Any attempt to analyze your own dreams according to this chart could lead to hysterical pregnancy. And you don't want one of those.

SYMBOL/MEANING

Blue, color
Issues of cognition, or logic, or possibly that it's a boy

Cars
Wish to escape; or wish to move more quickly; or wish that you could fit behind your own steering wheel

Crossing a river
A change in attitude

Diapers
Fear of changing diapers

Desert
Sandbox

Eating
Generalized wish fulfillment

Floating
Fear that you now resemble a hot-air balloon

Flying
Fear, specifically, that you now resemble the Sea World blimp

Mountains
Distant goal, separation

Old woman
Eternal female wisdom; or, to the contrary, fear that your mother-in-law will come to visit

Parallel parking
Resentment of having to "back and fill" or even execute difficult "K-turns" to exit from dining rooms of certain local restaurants

Stork
Diaper delivery service

Test, not being prepared for
Fear of labor

Trees
Hammock envy, probably connected to a strong wish to lie down

Underwear, going to school in your
Fear of same

Whales
Lamaze class

CHAPTER TEN
The Ninth Month

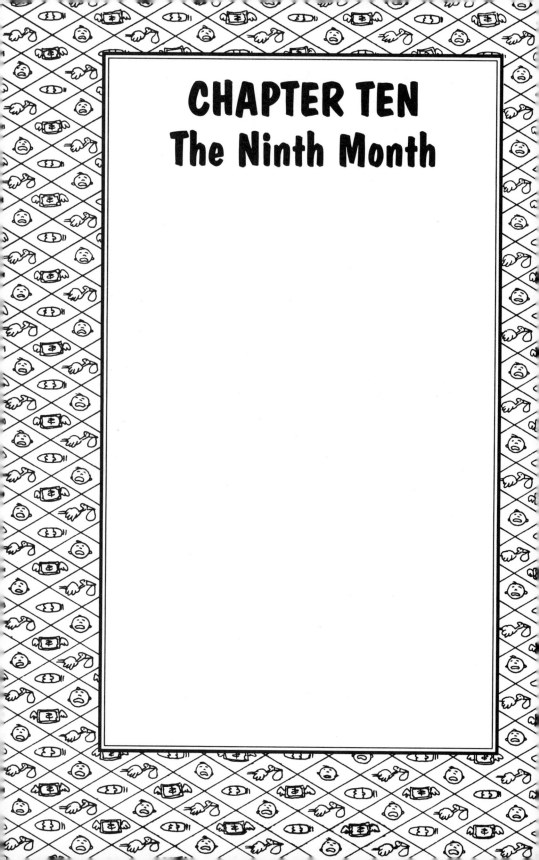

WHAT YOUR WIFE WILL BE COMPLAINING ABOUT

▶ Exhaustion

▶ You

▶ All men

▶ Feelings of disorientation

▶ Her weight

▶ That if it's false labor, it shouldn't be real pain

▶ Your weight

▶ Everything on the "What Your Wife Will Be Complaining About" lists for months one through eight

▶ That she needs an assistant to read the bathroom scale

▶ That bathtub is not deep enough anymore

▶ That even maternity wear no longer fits; she's down to exactly one dress that fits

▶ Braxton Hicks contractions

▶ That a double bed should be a queen; or the queen should be a king; or the king should really be a quarter-acre of firm mattress

▶ The color you painted the nursery, which now seems too dark

▶ Mr. Braxton, Mr. Hicks, and their children's children

▶ When you try to bring her breakfast in bed, the bed table—well, it doesn't quite work anymore

▶ Not getting a seat on the bus or subway

▶ Not being able to get up from seat on the bus or subway

▶ The decor of your home as the nesting instinct kicks in

▶ Automobile seatbelt now impossible to wear

▶ The color you repainted the nursery—it's too light

▶ People who tell her stories of very easy births

▶ People who tell her stories of very difficult births

▶ Anyone who talks about giving birth

▶ That Baby doesn't seem to know that the due date has passed

▶ Fear of in-laws sending baby clothes she will hate

▶ That you really shouldn't be painting inside the house so much, the fumes can't be good for the baby

▶ Emotional highs and lows, fear, ecstasy, anxiety, and elation, often all at the same time

A COUPLE OF THINGS TO SAY TO LET HER KNOW YOU'RE CARING, SENSITIVE, AND UP ON THE REQUIRED READING

1. "While Leboyer childbirth seems appealing, there is no firm scientific evidence to support the arguments made in the book *Birth Without Violence*."

2. "A non-stress test may seem like a pregnancy oxymoron, but it is called that to distinguish it from a stress test, which is essentially the same monitoring of the baby, with the added 'stress' being an oxytocin drip to set off contractions."

WHAT TO BUY THIS MONTH

The baby's got to eat, right? This is the month to get ready for the bottle or the breast.

Estimated Costs, Month Nine
Basics: Bottle $759, Breast $310
Basics plus extras: Bottle $1,959, Breast $1,510

Basics
BOTTLEFEEDING
Automobile bottle warmer (plugs into cigarette lighter)
Bottle brush for cleaning
Bottle drying rack
Bottle sterilizing pan
Bottles
Formula
Hypoallergenic formula (just in case)
Rubber nipples

BREASTFEEDING
Book on why breastfeeding is best
Breast pump
Nipple shield
Nursing bras
Nursing pads

BOTH METHODS
Birth announcements
Car seat, up to 25 pounds
Car seat, 25-40 pounds

Extras
Library of works on child-rearing and education: Jean Piaget, Maria Montessori, Jerome Bruner, Marvin comic strip compilations
Professional-quality baby scale—why wait for appointments with the pediatrician to see how much baby is gaining

WHAT YOUR WIFE MAY LOOK LIKE

Throughout the final month your wife will generally give up on any effort to preserve her dignity. She will adopt the full-scale unapologetic waddle, go with minimalist hair care, and finally don the jungle-print muu-*moo!* she swore she'd never wear. She alternates between wide-eyed hysteria and zombie-like stupor and takes off her shoes whenever she damn well pleases.

WHAT TO TAKE TO THE HOSPITAL

Her bag is filled with extra socks, bedclothes, hairbrush, and everything else, but don't forget that you're probably going to be stuck in the hospital for a while yourself. Pack your bag now. Here are some recommendations.

▶ A pillow, for nodding off in chairs.

▶ A pack of cards, for tossing into a hat from ten paces until your wife tells you to cut it out.

▶ Toothbrush, comb, fresh shirt, but not a razor—the unshaven look is *de rigueur* for new papas.

▶ Address book that includes all major relatives.

▶ A tennis ball, for giving excellent lower back massage, especially during back labor, and also for bouncing mindlessly off a wall until your wife tells you to cut it out.

▶ A small harmonica. Did you know that you can teach yourself to play a few simple tunes in just minutes?

▶ A beeper. Not so people can reach you, but so the security guards will take you for a doctor and not make you sign in every time you pass through the lobby.

▶ A handful of quarters in case of problems with the room phone. (Also good for tossing to see how close you can land them to the wall until your wife tells you to cut it out.)

▶ This book. In those final hours it's important to have a handy, reassuring reference work that includes everything you need to know about labor and delivery, so find one and take it along, too. This book, opened to about page 59, makes a handy eyeshade for catnaps.

▶ Food. She's chosen some nuts and dried fruit, but you need more than that to keep up your energy. Be sure to include the four basic food groups: fruits and vegetables (popcorn, ketchup, grape Kool-Aid); meats and fish (Slim Jims, pork rinds, Goldfish); cheese and dairy (Cheddar Cheese Goldfish, Cheeze Puffs, Milk Duds); and cereals and grains (Wheaties, Doritos, Tostitos, Pringles). Pop-Tarts also travel well, and fruit-filled Pop-Tarts encompass two essential food groups.

▶ Music—tapes or CDs. She'll ask for something soothing, but don't guess what that means; be sure to clear each choice *before* hitting the play button.

▶ Three stopwatches: one for timing contractions, one as an emergency backup, and one for timing how long you can hold your breath until your wife tells you to cut it out.

▶ Pencil and pen, for recording important thoughts, instructions, and things to do, and also for tossing up at the acoustic ceiling in an attempt to make them stick, until your wife says she'll throttle you with her bare hands, contraction or no contraction, if you come up with one more stupid stunt.

▶ An expensive, beautiful, and incredibly thoughtful gift for your wife. Always a good idea during times of high stress.

What You May Be Concerned About
CRIB NOTES LAMAZE

"I missed a lot of Lamaze classes. What do I absolutely need to know?"

Lamaze and other childbirth classes are much like high-school driver's education courses: They're not strenuous, it's better to sit in the back, and the one thing not to miss is the films.

Preparation for childbirth—for the father—should be focused on one basic goal: not fainting at the sight of your newborn. The films of childbirth, though lacking in compelling dialogue, have a solid dramatic structure and will teach you one simple lesson: The greenish, slimy, blood-streaked thing hanging upside down in the doctor's hands is, in fact, a perfectly healthy baby. The films aren't pretty, but keep your eyes open, because the real thing is no prettier.

Aside from the films, of course, you'll want to learn a few breathing techniques and the information about all the available painkilling options so that you'll know how to explain to your wife why "you're not doing anything to help!"

What You May Be Concerned About
THE BABY

"As the big day approaches, my anxieties are driving me crazy. I've just got to know that our baby is going to be okay."

Try to relax. You've eaten right, avoided all the problems you could, done everything you could to improve your odds. And while we can't guarantee that your baby will be perfect, we can guarantee that your baby will be ugly. Yup. Ugly is a sure thing when it comes to newborns.

Sure, everyone will coo and say how beautiful the baby is, but most of them are seeing the kid after three or four days of recovery and respiration. You, however, will be face-to-face with this creature the very first moment that he or she looks around and says, "What the . . . !"

As is well known, newborns looks like J. Edgar Hoover, Winston Churchill, or at best, the young Babe Ruth. However, the pudgy, wrinkled, droopy look is the least of it. Here are a few more reasons to keep photography to a minimum until a month has passed:

▶ The caput. An elegant name for a highly inelegant bump on the noggin.
▶ Sugar-loaf molding. Another pretty name, but how pretty can elongation of the head possibly be? The passage through the birth canal essentially squishes Baby's head into a point. "We are from France, feel free to consume mass quantities."

▶ Boxer's nose. Says it all.
▶ Baby rug syndrome. In an apparent effort to hide their baldness, some babies are born with an all-natural bad toupee. This hair, often dark, long, and patchy, will fall out eventually and be replaced by new growth.
▶ Lanugo. Yes, it was a dance sensation from the late eighties, but it's also patches of downy hair that occur in the oddest places on newborns.
▶ Blotches. Call them angel kisses if it makes you feel better, but there is a whole assortment of potential birthmarks that will keep any baby off the box front of Ivory Snow.
▶ Milia. Or, yes, baby acne. Life is unfair, right from the start. At least most teenagers deserve what they get.
▶ Receding chin and silly-looking mouth. Don't worry, teeth will eventually give this area a lot more structure and dignity. Have you seen Gramps without his dentures?

What You May Be Concerned About
COLD FEET

"I'm really concerned about keeping my cool during the delivery. I've never been too crazy about hospitals, and the sight of blood, IVs—I probably shouldn't go, right?"

Many men—indeed many people—feel uncomfortable in the hospital, and around the medical equipment and procedures involved in a modern birth. Perhaps you should consider home birth. Just kidding, but if we scared you, good. You can be thankful that you don't have any real responsibility in the hospital. The least you can do is tag along and not faint at the sight of her first blood test.

In many cultures, childbirth is the exclusive province of women. A mother, sister, or female friend is more likely to be present as the pregnant woman's companion. Too bad you don't live in one of those cultures. You will be mocked and ridiculed if you don't accompany your wife to the hospital. But if you are still concerned about being present, you and your wife should talk it over. Share your feelings, your fears and discomfort. You'll still have to go, of course, but maybe she'll forgive you if you proceed to nod off during the twenty-seven hours of early labor.

visits occur every half-hour, she has about two weeks to go. Finally, when she is so completely exhausted from getting up constantly that she asks if you'd mind if she wet the bed, you can zip up the hospital bag and call work, because the long wait is nearly over.

By the way, don't tell her she can, because she will, and you'll both regret it in the long run.

What You May Be Concerned About
THE DUE DATE

"The doctors don't seem all that sure of the due date. Is there any simple way of judging how far along we are?"

In fact, there is. Much as timing contractions can tell you how far along labor has progressed, timing your wife's trips to the bathroom can give an excellent estimate of your due date. When she needs to urinate every hour, you can be sure labor is a least a month away. When

CHAPTER ELEVEN
Labor and Delivery

WHAT YOUR WIFE WILL BE COMPLAINING ABOUT

▶ Exhaustion

▶ You

▶ Labor and childbirth

▶ That willpower seems to have no effect in making irregular contractions become regular

▶ Your timing contractions incorrectly

▶ That it's painful to walk; extremely painful to do anything else

▶ Pain

▶ Extreme pain

▶ That she can't decide when to go the hospital

▶ Your attempt to start her on Lamaze breathing techniques—it's too soon

▶ That there's no good reason to get total anesthesia

▶ That the nurse won't wait for the contraction to end before trying for the third time to hit a vein with the IV

▶ Lamaze

▶ The hospital room

▶ That she can't believe her ob-gyn is not on-call

▶ Her third-grade art teacher (logic has no meaning to a woman in labor)

▶ Peer pressure, which is keeping her from taking any and all available anesthetics

▶ It may not exactly be clear what she's complaining about, because it's hard to understand her through clenched teeth, but definitely not a happy face

▶ The doctors who don't seem to realize that no one has ever been in this much pain before

▶ Emotional highs and lows, fear, ecstasy, anxiety, and elation, often all at the same time

A COUPLE OF THINGS TO SAY TO LET HER KNOW YOU'RE CARING, SENSITIVE, AND UP ON THE REQUIRED READING

1. "You know a prolonged active phase can be caused by a malposition of the baby. Could be a breech, the head hasn't descended into the pelvis, or there is cephalopelvic disproportion—and we all know how much that can hurt, right honey?"

2. "Until the eighteenth century women never lay down to give birth; they would walk or stand or squat—all of which are physiologically superior positions. It was the obstetrician to the French court, a doctor named Mauriceau, who introduced the practice of lying down—and the court's standards were widely imitated. I'm sorry, were you having a contraction, honey?"

3. "You know, having the baby hurts, but apparently expelling the placenta afterwards doesn't hurt a bit. That's something to be thankful for, right honey?"

The Popgar Test

With the increased participation of fathers in the birthing process, with fathers even attending cesarean births, it became necessary to develop a hospital methodology for the fathers. The acronymic POPGAR test has become the norm. This simple test was developed in the late 1980s to help hospital personnel evaluate a father in those critical moments just after the birth of his child. He is rated on a scale of 0, 1, or 2 points, in six areas: Pallor, Optimism, Pride, Grimace, Activity, and Relatives. A total score of 7 or above indicates a healthy father; a low score may indicate a need for more careful observation.

How the POPGAR Test Is Scored

Area	0	1	2
Pallor	White as a sheet	Washed out	Pale
Optimism	Thinks baby said "Dada"	Thinks baby is looking at him	Thinks baby is beautiful
Pride	Asks nurse if the press has been bothering her for details	Asks nurse if she's ever seen a more perfect baby	Asks nurse if all babies are so great
Grimace	Slack-jawed	Smiles hazily	Can't stop grinning
Activity	Nods off in chair	Walks baby	Dances with baby
Relatives	Can't remember if he has relatives	Has called some relatives	Has called all relatives and many complete strangers

VIDEOTAPING YOUR DELIVERY

Until hospitals lift their overly conservative policies restricting the delivery room to the woman and her partner or coach, there is only one way to share the experience of your labor and delivery with family and friends: the magic of videotape.

Nowadays the purchase of a home video camera is as much a part of pregnancy as painting the nursery. So don't wait until you bring the baby home to begin the documentary drama of life. And for goodness sake, neither you nor your wife should be shy about taping these special hours for posterity. The camera may seem intrusive at times, and it's not always easy to think about your laboring wife's needs and keep an eye on the white balance levels at the same time, but the laughs you'll share when you watch with relatives and co-workers will more than make up for any initial feelings of embarrassment.

How to make a quality tape? Luckily, most modern hospital's delivery rooms are extremely well lit. Amateur videographers are thus protected from the most common problem, which is low light. You will probably need a standard video light for the hospital room itself, but once active labor begins—at which time you may be distracted from your camera-work—the lighting is all taken care of. Some expectant fathers worry that they simply cannot function effectively as both cameraman and coach. Well, that's what tripods are for! Should your wife need a quick review of breathing techniques or someone to toss a stray curse at, you can be there—and still be getting it all down on tape. Unfortunately, the resulting video will be rather static, and you risk losing your audience's full attention. You may want to consider doing what an acquaintance of ours did. He simply strapped his camcorder to a football helmet, creating a perfectly serviceable "Daddy-cam." A ten-dollar remote cable allowed him to operate the pause/record button with his teeth and still have both hands free for brow mopping and back rubbing.

When you're preparing to tape your child's birth, it is best to make everything as idiot-proof as possible, because with all the excitement and tension it's easy to forget to charge the batteries or create in-camera graphics. Here are some simple videotaping tips for in the delivery room:

▶ Don't ask the anesthesiologist to hold the microphone.
▶ Don't ad-lib a humorous voice-over as you shoot.
▶ Don't try to make the atmosphere seem "more personal" by asking the doctors and nurses to remove their masks.
▶ Never, ever tell your wife to push harder because you're running out of tape.
▶ Don't joke with the hospital personnel about the tape being good evidence for your upcoming malpractice suit.
▶ Don't video cesareans.

▶ Don't attempt a humorous postgame interview with your wife.

▶ Don't attempt to come up with similes to describe the moments-old newborn.

▶ Three hours is too long, even if you're planning to edit it down, and you'll never get around to editing it down, anyway.

▶ Ignore all of the above and anything in this book, or in any book, that suggests you videotape your wife's delivery. First, most hospitals won't let you. Second, you don't want to do this, trust me. Third, sure there's a lot you'd like to remember in labor and delivery, but there is also a lot you'll want to forget.

REAL ADVICE: WHAT YOU NEVER EXPECTED WHEN YOU'RE EXPECTING

Up to this point in this compendium of helpful guidance for expectant fathers we have made every effort to give advice that is flippant, inconsequential, and for the most part extraneous, if not irrelevant. However, out of a sense of duty and moral responsibility, we felt it was important to provide a modicum of *real* advice—genuine information that will point you and your wife toward a wonderful, enriching childbirth experience. Through diligent research we found these tidbits of reality—options in pregnancy, labor, and delivery for you to consider.

Invite Flipper
As reported in *USA Today* under the heading "Dolphin Births Nixed," a group of six British women were denied permission to deliver their babies in a special glass-walled water tank in the Red Sea. Their obstetrician hoped that being born among dolphins would give the infants a special affinity with nature, and might improve human–dolphin communication.

Invite the Neighbors
Unlike modern America, where laboring women are sequestered in hospitals, other societies have made birth a pleasant social affair. Family and friends—including children—gather to offer moral support for the young mother-to-be. Imagine all your nearest and dearest cheering you on through the entire labor and birth.

Technology from NASA
Though the system is not particularly popular, some countries have allowed the use of a special decompression suit for the laboring mother. This suit lifts the abdomen away from the uterus during each contraction. The decrease in pressure on the uterus allows it to work more effectively, which means less pain for the mother.

Only in Sweden
An innovation in natural childbirth has been pioneered in Sweden. Doctors there have found that using a Japanese-made cervical vibrator as often as three times during the first stage of labor allows the

cervix to relax between contractions. This, in turn, allows the cervix to work more effectively with the contractions.

What You May Be Concerned About
FEAR OF SWITCHING

"I watch a lot of made-for-television movies. I guess what I'm trying to say is that I know it's probably ridiculous, but I'm terrified the hospital will somehow switch our baby."

No fear that you are feeling is ridiculous, but you should be reassured by the simple fact that only one in ten babies born in this country is accidentally switched with another at the hospital. Nonetheless, fear of a switch crosses the mind of almost every new parent. Did we say one in ten? We meant one in ten million births, and actually we just made up that figure, but it's probably some really big number like ten or twenty million.

That said, it is still worth putting your mind at ease by taking a few simple precautions as soon as your child is born. One father we know spent a few moments bonding with his newborn, and after deciding that he couldn't focus on any particular distinguishing feature, he took a moment to put a simple black X on his child's foot. Sure, the nurses were a little mystified, and his wife teased him relentlessly, but at least he came home with *his* baby. An indelible marker, a friendship bracelet, a quick haircut, whatever you do, don't rely on memo-

rizing your baby's features. He may look unique at that first moment—and we're not saying that there was ever a baby so cute—but your perspective will be a little different when you're behind the glass of the hospital nursery looking at a whole roomful of squishy little faces.

What You May Be Concerned About
PAINKILLERS

"We're getting so much information about all the various options for pain relief—epidurals, analgesics, hypnosis— that it's dizzying. Aren't there any simple answers?"

Unfortunately, the process of labor and childbirth is a complicated matter, with many possibilities and probabilities to be considered. You may experience severe tension headaches, back strain, and even red, irritated eyes. When giving back massages, you may find that your arms cramp up. When you nod off in a chair, your leg may fall asleep, too, causing a painful tingling when you try to use it. It can't be denied: Childbirth involves pain.

Ideally, your childbirth preparation classes have taught you not to fear the pain. Though many of those classes focus on the woman's perspective, the same basic principles apply to you. Concentrate on your breathing. Use the pain; don't fight it so much as try to go with it. Most of all, relax as much as you can, whenever you can. If you can nod off between your wife's contractions, that's great.

Still, there comes a time for medical intervention and you shouldn't feel bullied into refusing it. Pay no attention to people who say that with medication you aren't "really experiencing" childbirth. If you need a couple of aspirin for the headache, take them, by all means. (And bring your own, because the hospital won't give out any medication to non-patients.) Feel free to do whatever you can to ease the pain during the long hours of labor and the intense pressure of childbirth. You deserve a little help in getting through it.

What You May Be Concerned About
WHAT TO SAY DURING LABOR

"We took the classes, I've read the books, and I'm still not exactly sure what I'm supposed to say or to do as labor coach, except that it has something to do with a tennis ball."

Many men go into labor—so to speak—terrified of saying the wrong thing and, in the midst of labor, are bored of saying the same thing over and over. And the tennis ball—suggested as a means of massaging the lower back—seldom actually comes into play.

What can you do? It's really not that complicated. First, you are your wife's willing slave, jumping at her every whim.

Second, you are an interpreter between your wife and the hospital personnel, explaining to her what they are suggesting, and translating her grunts and snarls into relatively polite discourse. Third is the coaching part—and don't worry, the nurses handle the nitty-gritty. You didn't really think that you would be the one to make the call on when active labor has begun, or when to administer an epidural, did you? So don't worry about keeping an eye on the readouts from the fetal monitor. Plus, the nurses most likely know all the breathing gimmicks better than you do. So all you really have to do is provide encouragement and love. How? Stick to the basics, and if in doubt, remember that especially as labor progresses, chitchat may only annoy—significant eye contact may be all she wants.

What to Say to Your Wife During Early (First-Phase) Labor
1. "Everything is packed and ready to go."
2. "I love you."
3. "I bought you a little present—just for being a wonderful person."
4. "I just have a feeling it's going to go smoothly."
5. Sing the complete lyrics to "You're Having My Baby" while the sense of humor is still functioning.
6. "It must have been that Chinese food."
7. "I hope she looks like you."
8. "Just try to relax as much as you can."

What NOT to Say to Your Wife During Early (First-Phase) Labor

1. "Just relax as much as you can—labor can go on for days."
2. "This isn't another bogus false labor thing is it?"
3. "I forget, which hospital is it again?"
4. "Either my stopwatch is broken or the contractions are slowing down."
5. "Can't we wait a little longer before we go to the hospital? It's the fourth quarter."
6. "Don't forget, this is the easy part."
7. "I just can't wait to have that baby."

What to Say to Your Wife During Active (Second-Phase) Labor

1. "I love you."
2. "That's great."
3. "Good, beautiful."
4. "You're wonderful."
5. "Sure it does."
6. "You're doing great."
7. "Relax between contractions—that's it."
8. "You can do it."
9. "You're strong."
10. "Is there anything at all you want?"

What NOT to Say to Your Wife During Active (Second-Phase) Labor

1. "You don't look like you're having fun." (Sarcasm might play during first-phase labor, but lose it for active labor.)
2. "You're not as relaxed as you should be." (Negativity.)
3. "I can't bear to see you in so much pain." (She needs strength not pity.)
4. "I just figured out in my head how much this hospital is costing us per minute."

5. "You had the baby! Made you look."
6. "You know, if you could hold off for just a couple more hours, then I could make the phone calls after eleven."
7. "You think this is tough? Larry's wife was in labor for forty-three hours."
8. "Mind if I nap until the action starts?"

What to Say to Your Wife During Transitional (Third-Phase) Labor

1. "It's okay, you're okay."
2. "I love you."
3. "You're wonderful."
4. "You're working hard."
5. "You're doing great."
6. "Remember, just relax between contractions—don't anticipate the next one."
7. "We've waited a long time—and that baby's not that far away now."

What NOT to Say to Your Wife During Transitional (Third-Phase) Labor

1. "A friend of mine who's a doctor said that physiological evidence shows that labor ranks right up there with gunshot wounds on the pain scale."
2. "I've heard that there's a kind of amnesia so that women don't remember just how painful labor was."
3. "Do you think I look nice in the hospital regulation outfit?"
4. "Once I broke my wrist and that sure hurt."
5. "I can't believe you haven't even broken your water yet."
6. "Look, the baby! Just kidding."
7. "I've been having some second thoughts about the name we decided on."
8. "Don't blame me—it's nature."

9. "Do you ever wonder how competent all these doctors and technicians are?"

10. "Well, if you're not going to breathe with me, I'm just not going to bother breathing at all."

What to Say to Your Wife During Pushing, Delivery, and After

1. Nothing until after—she's not listening.
2. "You did it."
3. "You're wonderful."
4. "I love you."
5. "Look at our baby boy/girl."
6. "Thank you."

What NOT to Say to Your Wife During Pushing, Delivery, and After

1. "It's great that you're not worried about your modesty anymore."
2. "Look at what a mess this place is."
3. "You know what's another good name for a girl? Sylvia—isn't that a pretty name?"
4. "Eww—that's the baby?"
5. "Yes, I did it!"
6. "When can we have another one?"
7. "Wait a minute, that baby looks like Phil, our garage mechanic."
8. "How many days do you think you want to stay—two, three?"
9. "What should I do with all the dirty laundry at home?"

What You May Be Concerned About
TAKING PICTURES

"I was talked out of videotaping our upcoming birth, but I'd like to take some photographs. Are there any problems with still photography in hospitals?"

Our advice is quite simple: Take your camera to the hospital but do not take any pictures until one full hour after the birth of your child. Any photographs of your wife in labor will not be appreciated; photographs of deliveries are best confined to pregnancy guides and medical textbooks; and newborns look a lot better once they've had a little breathing room. Also, go with high-speed film so that you can minimize flashes in your baby's eyes during the first hours of life. This is not for physiological reasons but for psychological ones. Taking too many photos can give the hour-old child an inflated sense of importance (infant paparazzo syndrome).

What You May Be Concerned About
CIRCUMCISION

"I always assumed that circumcision was done for medical reasons, but now I hear that it is no longer considered particularly beneficial."

Fathers who have attended their baby's circumcision are usually shocked to see what he has to go through. They often feel guilt and anguish over having authorized the procedure. This is a very good reason not to go and watch. Do you really want to see your newborn son placed in a "circumstraint" and see a hemostat applied, clamps, and . . . you don't even want to read about it.

Does it hurt? Are you kidding? It hurts just thinking about it. Some people tell themselves that the infant's nervous system is not fully developed. These people are fooling themselves. For certainly most little boy infants wail when the deed is done.

Is it worth doing? The most common reason that 80 percent of parents still choose circumcision is that 80 percent of parents still choose circumcision. This fear of looking different may be unfortunate, but it is not unreasonable. Looking different from your father can also be confusing for a young boy. The argument, based solely on aesthetics, that somehow it just looks better is basically a cover for the fact that 80 percent of baby boys start life with a little trim.

Of course, you may be Jewish. If you're not sure, don't worry about it. If you are, circumcision is more than just a little hospital procedure, it's a briss. This means you must wait the traditional eight days, then have a moil come remove in a special service what the forefathers had removed. Relatives and friends gather in joyous celebration, complete with lox-and-bagel platters, while the little fellow and his mother are in the back bedroom sobbing. By the way, if you're Christian and feeling left out, you could celebrate the Circumcision (of Jesus, that is) which is January 1, although not many churches hold special services. And if they did, what exactly would they be praying for?

Rumors about circumcision's role in human sexuality are common but unfounded. It has never been proven that circumcised men can hold an erection longer, nor has it been proven that uncircumcised men experience greater sexual pleasure, although a government-funded group of researchers at the University of Michigan had a hell of good time trying to establish one or the other.

CHAPTER TWELVE
The First Weeks

WHAT YOUR WIFE WILL BE COMPLAINING ABOUT

▶ Exhaustion

▶ You

▶ Why does she still look pregnant if Baby is out?

▶ That she will never walk again—despite nurses' continual "you'll recover faster" urging to try

▶ Perineal pain

▶ Fear of postpartum depression (technically known as pre-postpartum depression)

▶ Fear of bowel movements

▶ Sore nipples if breastfeeding

▶ Engorgement if not breastfeeding

▶ Whoever invented breastfeeding in the first place?

▶ That you just don't understand

▶ Your family's visits, gifts, comments, attitude

▶ The flowers—she doesn't want to leave any behind

▶ Nurses—they're patronizing

▶ Nurses—they never tell her anything

▶ That she did all the work; you get half the credit

▶ That she initially felt that Baby was the most gorgeous cherub ever; now realization of baby's plug-ugliness is dawning

▶ Baby's bellybutton stump, which she finds really gross

▶ That Baby is already too big for the Philadelphia Eagles jumper you bought, although it's probably just as well

▶ Name you agreed on, which suddenly seems wrong

▶ That Social Security already wants to give your baby a number—it's creepy

▶ That Baby doesn't understand plain English

▶ That Baby doesn't understand the concept of "night"

▶ Emotional highs and lows, fear, ecstasy, anxiety, and elation, often all at the same time

A COUPLE OF THINGS TO SAY TO LET HER KNOW YOU'RE CARING, SENSITIVE, AND UP ON THE REQUIRED READING

1. "Hey look, I know what that is, that's meconium!"

2. "Sure our baby looks a little yellow, but it's just mild jaundice. Thank goodness he doesn't have hemolytic jaundice from blood incompatibility—which could damage the nervous system."

3. "Watch—I can get the baby to do the Moro reflex, just by dropping her."

4. "Did you know that the discovery of the hand—a baby noticing its own hand—is one of the essential steps toward psychomotor coordination?"

WHAT DID YOU EXPECT?

It will come as a shock, but when you get home from the hospital, you'll realize that being pregnant was easy. Especially for you, the expectant father. Oh sure, there were a lot of inconveniences, minor aches and pains, nettlesome planning, and some baby furniture to assemble, but all of it cannot compare to the early days of fatherhood.

Pregnancy is neat and contained. Fatherhood is all over the place. The baby's in the bassinet, the bottles are boiling, the baby needs a change, your wife would love a cup of tea, the baby needs a change, the two A.M. feeding, the four A.M. feeding, the desperate five A.M. drive around the block, the baby needs a change and in the middle of it puts on a stunning free-form aerial demonstration and the baby and you need a change, "Good morning, we're out of coffee," the diaper service deliveryman is at the door, time to make the doughnuts. And off to work with you.

You suddenly feel nostalgic for morning sickness. Remember when days would go by without much more than a "Oh feel here, honey, she's kicking!" or an awkward attempt to give a back rub to someone who is all front? And when you went to sleep you could sleep until morning. Didn't even seem that special, sleeping till morning. You know, just close your eyes, drift off, wake up in the morning. "Good night, see you in the morning." Just one night! Just one night straight through! Is that so much to ask!?

Relax. Sleep deprivation, with its attendant psychoses and hallucinations, is a perfectly natural part of early parenting. Many experts on early childhood and parenting experts agree that only by this "disassociation from reality" can the parent survive the trauma of the first six months.

What You May Be Concerned About
CRYING

"Crying at night, crying first thing in the morning, I can't take it anymore—and the baby cries a lot too. And what should I do when the baby and wife are both crying? Who should I go to first?"

You might think that babies cry all the time, and that a crying adult would always be first priority, but think again. If you go to your wife to console her, the howling of the baby will only make you both so tense and anxious that you'll end up snapping, "Quit blubbering" and she'll say, "You don't deserve a family because you don't care about anyone but yourself," and the baby will still be screaming like a banshee with a hot foot, and she'll say, "Just go away, you make me sick," and you'll say, "Nothing would make me happier than to leave you and your misery," and then you'll go get the baby finally, and your wife will still be crying or possibly calling her mother, or even a lawyer, and it turns out that the baby had her arm stuck in the side of the crib and now you feel really bad, the baby hates you, the wife hates you, and you've got to get up in the morning, don't forget.

What You May Be Concerned About
TAKING CARE OF MOM

"I run my own business and can't afford to stay home from work for too long, but I want to take good care of my wife too."

More and more men are available during those first weeks, thanks to paternity leave specifically and male enlightenment in general, but for some it won't be possible. If your wife buys your particular excuse, you're past the biggest hurdle, but you'll still want to arrange some kind of help for her.

The first option is, of course, her mom. You probably don't have much choice in this matter. If they've worked it out, Mom will be waiting on the doorstep when you bring the baby home. And if you've never appreciated your mother-in-law, you will now. An extra nap and a warm meal never looked so good. You'll probably forgive her for everything. Of course, when the baby is learning to walk, it might be time to suggest politely that she is pushing the limits of her welcome.

Another option is your mom. Just kidding.

Finally, if you can afford a small luxury, look for a *doula* service. It's a

Greek term meaning "to mother the mother," which seems like a lot for one word, but then those Greeks have a very impressive-looking alphabet. The people who provide this service are usually RNs or LPNs, but in addition to taking care of the baby and instructing the new mom, they are a sympathetic companion for her, do light housekeeping, even cooking and laundry. If you can't be there, at least you should feel guilty enough to offer to fork over the moolah for the *doula*.

What You May Be Concerned About
HAIR LOSS

"Maybe I'm imagining it, but I think I'm losing hair more rapidly."

There is still disagreement in the medical community over this issue. Pregnancy—and postpartum in particular—is a traumatic period for the father, both emotionally and physically. Could this cause hair loss and accelerated balding?

Women in the postpartum period will also suffer hair loss, but this is definitely a temporary physiological experience. High hormone levels during pregnancy cause hairs that would ordinarily fall out to stay. Her hair will get thicker throughout the nine months, but with childbirth, decreases in those hormone levels will cause the extra hair to fall out. This is a natural process that may be shocking, but it does not lead to baldness.

In men the news is not so cheery. Hair loss is hair loss, like it or not. Could trauma be at the root of the problem? Most scientists believe that balding is solely determined by genetics, others believe that physical and emotional factors have an effect, and a small minority believe that tiny hair elves come and pluck at the scalps of men who have been bad.

There is hope. The national epidemic of balding is beginning to get the public attention and scientific funding it deserves. Many old theories of balding are now being tested in research labs. The it's-determined-by-your-mother's-father's-hair genetic theory has been disproved by the author; our forehead is ever-heightening, while Grandfather sported his shock of dignified white hair all his seventy-seven years. The promulgators of such theories should think twice about the false confidence they inspire—and about our broken hearts, damn it.

Other theories have also been put to rest. Does hat wearing cause baldness? Definitely not, although researchers have established that balding does cause hat-wearing. Conspiracy theorists who believe that the International Hair Club for Men has put something into the nation's water supply have yet to produce hard evidence.

Pregnancy? There is no definite link, but at least one group of researchers have found a correlation between high hormone levels in women and balding in their husbands. They note, however, that this is a preliminary finding and open to interpretation.

Our advice is not to worry too much. You'll still have more hair than the baby, for a few months anyway.

What You May Be Concerned About
FEAR OF CHANGING

"I don't like changing diapers. Can we start toilet training now that the baby is a week old?"

No, you may not, you sniveling wimp. You're so far away from toilet training, it's funny. But the most-feared task in fathering is also the most overrated. Changing diapers is no big deal. In the first two years of life you will become completely inured to many grosser tasks. If you want something to feed your nightmares, try these:

▶ Taking the baby's temperature with the rectal thermometer.

▶ Sucking snot out of the baby's nose with a nasal aspirator.

▶ We don't even want to talk about it— but it has to do with constipation.

▶ Catching vomit in your hand, because you didn't have a spit-up diaper handy.

▶ Blowing baby's nose with your bare hand, using either a discreet fling or a sock for disposal.

▶ Using your own former toothbrush to clean a wicker chair that met up with a leaky diaper.

It would be irresponsible to go into detail about the potential disasters that loom, but we give one simple warning: Never play flying baby lying on your back with your mouth open right after the baby has been fed.

All that said, if changing diapers still gets you down, think about this short conversation that a recent father had with his local diaper service. (We join the conversation in progress.)

FATHER: But we returned all seventy diapers, and you only dropped off fifty.

SERVICE: If your standing order is for seventy, then a hundred and forty diapers are in circulation.

FATHER: Yes, but I promise you we aren't hoarding diapers, but need seventy delivered.

SERVICE: Are you double-diapering?

FATHER: Uh, yes, at night.

SERVICE: Make sure to separate them when you put them in the pail.

FATHER: Separate them?

SERVICE: When they spread out the diapers to be counted on the conveyer through the electric eye, the people that separate them sometimes miss some if they're stuck together.

FATHER: Oh.

SERVICE: Is there anything else we can help you with? Sir? Hello?

FATHER: Oh . . . uh, good-bye.

SERVICE: Bye.

Yes, there are people somewhere

who go in to work every Monday morning at an assembly line where they separate dirty diapers. Think about that the next time you see your wife squinch up her nose and call out, "It's your turn."

THE NAME

"I can't get used to the name we gave this baby. It just doesn't seem to be sticking. Is it possible we picked the wrong name?"

Many new parents can't get used to the idea that they can just give this new creature a name. Assigning a name, after all, is a quintessential expression of power. Adam—the first man—was given the task of naming all the other creatures.

If you knew your baby's gender and picked a name months ago, it may seem more natural to you. It is simply a matter of finally making a formal introduction. But if you're one of those who waited, laying a name on this baby may seem impossible. What if Baby doesn't like it?

Have you really chosen the wrong name? Impossible! You considered, you debated, you settled on the name you both thought was right. Stick with it. (Actually, it is statistically possible—about one in twenty thousand—that you have chosen a name so bad that it is wrong, like Phlegma or Tohmas. In these cases the courts are very lenient and allow name changes with a minimum of legal entanglements.) The name you have chosen is the right one, but getting used to it can still be difficult. A silly nickname is often the answer. By calling your infant Fluffernutter or Baldy for a while, you can adjust yourself to the idea that the little ball of pudge is Cynthia, Gilbert, or Ariadna. And if you never really do get used to the name, the worst thing that can happen is that you'll end up with a twenty-five-year-old daughter in medical school who still goes by the name Fluffy.

WISDOM OF THE FATHERS

"Now that the baby is here and happy and healthy I've got a whole new set of anxieties. Number one is: who am I to teach this little bundle of joy all about the meaning of life?"

You've learned to be a decent friend: concerned, engaging, sympathetic. You've started learning to be a decent spouse: sharing, loving, supportive. But a father has to be all that and also *wise*. Whether you have any wisdom to offer or not, someday your child will ask—expecting reasonably complete, comprehensible answers—if dogs go to heaven, why there is war, what function belly buttons have, why some people are poor, why are they allowed to sell cigarettes if they're bad for you, why it isn't stealing when you take pencils and paper from the office.

How can you prepare for the interrogations? Who am I to tell you how to prepare? Reread the back cover: no promises of wisdom. So far, personally, I've gone with either misdirection—"Wanna see a neat magic trick"—or deflection "ask your mother." If we ever get around to the source-of-babies line of questioning, I'm planning to go full bore with the antiquated birds and bees, pollen and stamens metaphor. Not to save myself embarassement, mind you, I just hate to give away the ending of the health class films.

Looking out for number one is more than just good changing table advice. From day one, you've got to instill a winning attitude in your infant. After all, nice babies finish last. So push your kids! Teach them how to maneuver office politics, dress them for success, make them remember the full name of everyone they meet (to better win friends and influence people), show them how to properly fold a business letter, let them eat the olives from your martinis, give them every possible privilege, and of course, teach them not to take no for an answer.

You'll get just the kids you deserve.

What You May Be Concerned About
SUCCESS

"I don't want to push my kid, but I do want to make sure that he's stimulated and enriched and . . . all right, I do want to push my kid, okay?"

Everybody wants their baby to grow up happy and generous, socially graceful and successful, well-educated, with a profession, impressive titles, advanced degrees, loads of money, world travel, wonderful spouse, perfect grandchildren. You want for them all the things you can brag about. Everybody wants these things, but only the people who want them most will get them. The future is now. What will you teach your baby today? Who will they be tomorrow?

CHAPTER THIRTEEN
Life with Baby

WHAT YOUR WIFE WILL BE COMPLAINING ABOUT

- Exhaustion
- You
- That Baby smiled at her but everyone insists that it's just gas
- Sleep deprivation
- Breastfeeding—though easier now, it's still not exactly fun
- Breast pump
- Spit-up
- Diapers
- Fears of inadequacy as a mother
- Hospital bills, paperwork
- Inadequacy of local public schools
- The injustice of it all
- Poor quality of daytime television
- The high cost of college education
- That clipping a baby's fingernails terrifies her
- That her sister's baby has more hair
- That her sister's baby loves her car seat
- That Baby's beautiful blue eyes are quickly fading to brown
- Ridiculously high-pressure educational programs (French for Tots, Math Readiness, Baby Swimmers, etc.)
- Expense of same
- Birthmark that "would fade" but hasn't
- That doctor gave the baby an "outie"
- Black and white high-contrast educational toys—they're ugly
- Too many stuffed animals already
- Brain not working
- Designated-hitter rule (okay, but wouldn't it be cool if she did?)
- Emotional highs and lows, fear, ecstasy, anxiety, and elation, often all at the same time.

A COUPLE OF THINGS TO SAY TO LET HER KNOW YOU'RE CARING, SENSITIVE, AND UP ON THE REQUIRED READING

Remember, these suggestions are based on actual scientific studies.

1. "You know, another good reason that breastfeeding is preferable to the bottle is that breast milk has twice as much taurine, a nonprotein nitrogen compound, as there is in cow's milk (which is what most formulas are composed of). Taurine seems to be a necessary neurotransmitter or neuromodulator, and not only do babies have a limited enzymatic capacity for synthesizing taurine from precursors, but premature infants have been shown to have high concentrations of taurine in their blood, and I don't have to tell you what that means."

2. "Projectile vomiting—that is, vomiting that travels some distance away from the baby—though a bit terrifying, isn't a sure sign of a problem unless it happens frequently, once or twice every day."

3. "While constipation is a common problem in babies, it is very treatable, with the very rare exception of Hirschsprung's disease, a total constipation caused by malfunctioning intestinal muscles. I wonder if Mrs. Hirschsprung thought it was a good idea to give it the family name?"

4. "Did you know that more pediatricians are now warning against teaching babies to swim, not because of the danger of drowning, but because of the danger of water intoxication which happens when a baby—who doesn't know any better—drinks large amounts of water while in the pool, causing potentially serious imbalances internally."

WHAT TO BUY DURING THE FIRST YEAR

Just because you've been spending money all pregnancy long doesn't mean you can quit now. There's so much more your child needs, today!

Estimated Costs, The First Year
Basics: $1,235
(Does not include either diaper service at $60 per month or disposables $75 per month)
Basics plus extras: $6,285

Basics
Baby sunglasses
French for Tots
Gymboree classes
Home hair-cutting kit
Infant CPR classes, for you
Music time
Name in hand-tooled wood blocks
Professional portrait photos
Shoelace clamps (keeps 'em tied)
Spill-proof Cheerio/raisin dispenser
Toddler leash
Wee Playhouse acting workshops

Extras
Baby's own business cards
Baby's own home computer
Dog for Baby
Horseback riding lessons
New VCR—for after Baby forces "Mickey" into tape opening and fries internal circuitry
Nicer pajamas/bathrobe—since you're wearing them out of the house when for sleep-inducing drives
Tree house

TOTAL CHILDPROOFING

Making your home or apartment safe for your new child isn't as complicated as you may believe. Yes, there are childproofing services that will survey your home, make recommendations and installations, but nothing they do takes more than a little research, a bit of common sense, and the most basic carpentry. Sure, there are whole catalogs full of childproofing equipment, but you only need to buy what your home requires. How much does your home require? Where should you draw the line on childproofing? The final decision is your own.

There are certain basics that should be considered essential—outlet plugs, window gates, locks for the kitchen cabinets—beyond these items, each couple needs to find a level of comfort. If additional gates and baby monitors in every room make you feel secure, and thus help you relax, then they've accomplished something before your baby even comes home from the hospital.

If you know you want Total Childproofing you can call in consultants—they're in your local yellow pages—or do it yourself with the following products.

The Kitchen: Where Disaster Lurks

Dishwasher "Dummy" Control Panel
Because these controls are by far the most fascinating to the toddler, it may be worth installing a false front with knobs and levers they can adjust at will.

Floor Stubbies
Small rubber knobs glued onto the floor add traction to otherwise slick linoleum.

Combination Lock Knife Block
A simple four-number code allows you to remove knives.

Childproof Dogfood/Catfood Dish
Miracle device prevents your child from tasting Spot's dinner but allows the pooch to eat at will.

The Bathroom

Childproof Toilet Lid
Safe for kids, and fun at parties, when guests can't figure out the four-step unlocking mechanism.

Gentle Flush System
Patented commode soundproofing cushions and minimizes the loud and potentially frightening sound of the toilet flushing. Why should toilet training be any scarier than it already is?

Medicine Cabinet Lock 'n' Stor
Medicines are simply too dangerous to keep in the home. This national chain of warehouses will rent you a small medicine cabinet far across town, five or six flights up, and double-locked so that you and a Lock 'n' Stor employee must both be present with keys.

Toilet Paper Sensor
Alarm sounds when more then five feet of toilet paper is unrolled all at once.

The Dollopator
Automatically dispenses a single dollop of toothpaste, and no more, until reset by an adult. Crest is not, after all, a dessert topping.

For All Around the House

VCR Lock
Prevents small fingers from reaching in, from putting small items or food inside the machine, and from recording episodes of *Sharon, Lois and Bram's Elephant Show* over your tapes of the 1986 World Series.

Bicycle Helmets
Not just for cycling anymore! How many bumps on the noggin will your children suffer before you realize that this light, impact-absorbing shell with Velcro chin fastener should be the first thing they put on in the morning.

Choke Tester Tube
New and improved version no longer

includes removable lid that proved to be a hazard for children three and under.

SprayCoat (patent pending)

A simple one-step answer to all your childproofing needs. SprayCoat technicians cover every inch of your home with a soft, thick but transparent polymer. There'll be no hard edges anywhere, cleanups are a breeze, and you can stop feeling guilty about all the unread books on your shelves because they're permanently sealed in place.

Wall Switch Guard

Not strictly a safety item, but it will prevent kids from discovering how much "fun" it is to flick lights on and off incessantly.

Industrial Metal Lathe Safety Guards

Don't you hate it when you have to shut down your high-speed industrial lathe, just because Junior has toddled into the den? Not a problem with our six-step system that includes a child-size welder's mask, a flameproof baby jumper tested at six hundred degrees, and "Don't Touch the Rotating Metal Rod" signs.

Electrical Cord Camouflage

You've tried taping them down, buying covers, even living without electricity. Now try decorating those troublesome electrical cords with our *trompe l'oeil* paint kit to make them blend into wood floors, carpets, even the most intricate oriental rugs.

Alarms

Natural Gas Detector

Why let your home turn into a massive ticking time bomb?

Pool Alarm

When the pool water is disturbed, it goes off. Great for knowing when it has started raining, or when wind is blowing.

TV Radiation Monitor

Measures levels that will help minimize the damage of television radiation. (Plus, we've found that when sitting forty feet from the set, kids lose interest sooner and watch less television.)

WHAT TO EXPECT IN YOUR MAILBOX

If you think that J. Crew and L.L. Bean catalogs are putting wear and tear on your mailbox, prepare yourself for the postpartum postal deluge. As soon as America's legal conspiracy—mail order marketing lists—registers that you have been blessed with a bouncing baby consumer, the catalogs will come.

They know you will buy. Even more than chamois shirts and humorous boxer shorts, even more than Victoria's secrets (what exactly is she keeping a secret? I've looked through the catalog again and again and I still don't know), and even more than sharpening our image, we as a nation are willing to spend money on our kids. Recession or depression, our instinct to provide takes over. Even as we drive that '84 Toyota into the ground, clip coupons, tuck Tupperware into the briefcase, and take vacation in the backyard, we are still willing to recite the magic number (and expiration date) to an operator so that the kids can each have "a wooden puzzle of their own first name."

Or an adorable lavender-and-mint jumpsuit from *Hanna Andersson*. Or a couple of pairs of those "Sara's Prints" pajamas from *Children's Wear Digest*—the ones that aren't actually pajamas because the government won't allow plain cotton items to be sold as sleepware because it's not fire-retardant, but you know and we know that they *are* pajamas. While we're getting 100% cotton, let's get a couple of those "onesies" for infants from *The Natural Baby Catalog* and a few sweatshirts from *Playclothes* (and where can you get baby "workclothes?")—or maybe the sweatshirts in *After the Stork* are better, or cheaper? We'll take both. And that summer bonnet on the cover of *Hand in Hand: Choices for Children* is a must—and practical, really, babies have to cover up in the summer sun. Say, is that the *Disney Catalog*? Hit me with a couple of videos, and the Donald Duck slippers, don't babies need slippers? *F.A.O. Schwarz?*—classic—we'll take whatever's hot. Babar? Beautiful, gimme a couple stuffed and a couple wind-up.

Are we spoiling this baby? Let's see what we can get that'll really be good for them. Ah ha, we'll take the metric number rods from *Early Learning Center*, the marble run from *Sensational Beginnings*, the big block set, no not that one, the really big one from *Constructive Playthings*, something from *The Right Start*—whatever, it just sounds like a good place to order—and *The Great Kids Company*—send us two of your finest dress-up outfits and throw in some face paints. *Hearthsong?* Some fingerpaints or fingerpuppets or both. That should do it for now.

Oh wait, we didn't order anything from *Back to Basics Toys*. Hello? Do you have Erector Sets? You do! Okay . . .

What You May Be Concerned About
GOING BACK TO WORK

"Can I go back to work yet?"

Ah, yes, work. The halcyon place where coffee breaks are not broken dreams—they actually happen. A place where screaming, wailing, sobbing, and moaning are reserved for those infrequent discussions of salary. Most important of all, a place where each individual is responsible for his or her own bathroom needs. It's a place full of grown-ups, peace, and quiet.

And no, you can't go back to work. You've got time off, mister. You've come a long way, baby. Paternity leave is more and more common, thanks to more flexible work schedules, more progressive corporate attitudes, and management's realization that a man who isn't sleeping though the night is a liability anyway. When it all seems to be too much, remember that before long—a few weeks, at most a few months—you'll be back in the rat race, the lovely, predictable, satisfying nine-to-five. Your wife can take care of the home front. Or best of all, you can both go back to work and hire someone to raise your children. Remember, never *ever* say, even jokingly, that you'd love to stay home and be the primary caretaker. Sure, it'll make you sound hip, but you may later have the words *verbal contract* flung in your face.

What You May Be Concerned About
SAFETY CAN BE FUN

"We've childproofed every last corner of our home, but when I look at some of the toys we've got, frankly, I get scared. How can we know what's safe?"

After childproofing your home, it would be foolish to outfit your child with toys that are basically death-traps—things like balloons (choking hazard) and wooden blocks (sharp edges, weight); so be sure to use common sense in choosing playthings. It's not easy to find toys that are truly, thoroughly safe, but here are four basic items that we especially recommend for the safety-conscious parent.

No-Go Bike.
Looks just like the real thing, but your kids can push the pedals all day long without risky movement.

Sponge Blocks.
Old-fashioned wooden blocks are too hard, and these stack almost as well and double as cleaning accessories for those major spills.

Teddy Bore.
What's the danger in traditional stuffed animals? Kids can get too attached to their favorite, dragging it everywhere and drooling on it, among other things, and this can create a sanitary disaster area of a toy. The Teddy Bore is specially designed and thoroughly tested; he will not have any lasting appeal to most children. His humorless expression, scratchy surface, and faint mildewy odor guarantee it.

Look-Like-a-Book.
Why risk paper cuts?! It looks just like a book—but has no real pages or dangerously thin sheets of paper.

What You May Be Concerned About
FLYING BABIES

"We really want to take our baby to my parents for Christmas, but that means a long airplane flight. When will the baby be ready to fly? And what can we do to prepare?"

The one great thing about flying with an infant is that for once, your appearance with baby in your arms will *not* be greeted with oohs and aahs of admiration. As you walk down the aisle, all eyes will be upon you, but the looks will communicate pure terror, dread that your seat will be near. It's a pleasant change.

Actually, traveling with an infant is much easier than traveling with babies six months or older, on up to about fourteen years of age. By that time, your child will simply remain sullen and quiet, hoping that no one will think you are traveling together. Up until that age, anything can happen. An infant may be lulled to sleep by the plane's vibration and the white noise of the engines. Or the baby will scream holy murder from start to finish.

Now, if babies were meant to fly they would have been born with more fully developed inner ear systems. As it is, uncomfortable air pressure during descent and ascent affects them more than it does adults. Prepare a bottle and have it ready, as swallowing can alleviate the discomfort. Another handy tip: Teach your two-month-old infant how to chew gum, which will both ease the

pressure and give a charming "tough kid" look.

What You May Be Concerned About
SUPERMAN SYNDROME

"We've heard all about the modern day 'superwoman' juggling career and motherhood, but what about us? Am I wrong in feeling that I've fallen into a Superman Syndrome—trying to do it all?"

We may be going out on a limb, but it's fair to say that trying to balance family and career can be just as difficult for a man as for a woman. Maybe *more* difficult. Yeah, more difficult, that's it. The pressures and expectations are just too much—we have no role models. Our own fathers were absent, misinformed, and probably both. Today's father drives himself crazy trying to be the perfect supportive and dedicated husband, the merciless career juggernaut at work, and still a loyal pal to the boys in the poker circle.

It's up at four A.M. on Saturday to go trout-fishing, back to the house by nine to make waffles, then you've got to get the groceries and do the laundry in time to sit back and enjoy the afternoon's ballgame. A quick jog, so you don't go completely to pot, whip up a stew for dinner, do the dishes, repair that kitchen drawer that keeps falling out, repaint the bathroom, and then run out and rent a movie to watch together that evening.

It's one thing after another, and all to-gether, too exhausting.

When the baby comes, you will simply have to make choices. No man can be a scratch golfer and bake from scratch, too. And golfing is more fun than baking. So relax. You'll just have to settle for second best now and then. You can't "do it all" so don't try. Be ready to compromise now and then. If you need to stay late at the office, stay, she'll understand. If you need to take the boys from the office out to a great batting cage, she'll understand. But cut a few corners at work, too. Try making a short phone call to your wife from work, just to see how she's doing—the few minutes you lose won't cost you that promo-tion—and it would mean a lot to her. There are plenty of ways to show her you care. You could cash in your chips and leave the poker game in time to get home for the two A.M. feeding, just for one example.

Little things like that mean a lot to a new mother. And if all the pressures just seem to be too much, hit the panic button and escape. Think: When was the last time you did something just for you? Take a weekend "off" from the homefront and play thirty-six holes of golf. The more relaxed and happy you are, the better a helpmate you'll be when you *are* around. Right?

Oh well, they seemed like good ideas to us.

What You May Be Concerned About
CHILD CARE

"Life is so complicated with the new baby here, I haven't had time to begin looking for a live-in nanny. And, of course, we're concerned about making a good choice."

What do you want? Sympathy? Why don't you have the butler make a few phone calls for you, set up some inter-views with your personal secretary, and once they've got it down to two or three candidates, you can set down your drink by the pool and come inside for long enough to pick one. That shouldn't be too much of a strain.

Actually, that's not fair. Today more and more women with middle-class in-comes find that they must go back to work so that they can afford to pay for full-time child care. All right, that's still not fair because many women do need to work for economic reasons, and any woman certainly has the right to com-bine work and motherhood.

The choice between being a work-ing mother and working as a mother is a difficult one, and the two camps are breaking out into what has become a national "Mommy War." Basically women on both sides try to keep an open mind, but simply have no idea how the other side could possibly have made such a limiting, impractical, and essen-tially wrong decision. What is the husband's role? We'll give you a clue: It is *not* to carefully consider and weigh the pluses and minuses of each position. All right, we'll give you another clue. *Don't even come close to forming an opinion until your wife has made up her mind, then totally agree with her.* There's a war going on out there, and loose lips sink ships.

What You May Be Concerned About
POSTPARTUM MEDICAL SCHOOL SYNDROME

"My wife just had a baby and now she has decided she wants to go to medical school and become a doctor. She seems quite serious about this. Will it wear off?"

It may seem strange, but in fact, your situation is becoming more and more common. Postpartum medical school syndrome occurs in varying degrees in one out of four new mothers. For some, it is only a bothersome regret that they didn't pay more attention in tenth grade biology. For others, it leads to years of training and an M.D.

Why does it happen? Well, a little knowledge is a dangerous thing. Your wife has done nine months of intensive reading in pregnancy books, which present detailed medical information and are also full of criticism of the male hegemony in the medical profession which is blamed for everything from the high rate of cesareans to the parking problems around the hospital.

After all this research into medical possibilities, options in anesthesia, hospital regulations, and obstetrical innovations, your wife—no matter what her career up to this point—will feel that she missed her true calling and that she must become a doctor. So you are not alone, and it is certainly foolish to oppose your wife's wishes. Why try to stop her when the complexities of first-year biochemistry will probably do the job, without all the emotional underpinnings, the failure to be supportive, and all that?

And if she does become a doctor, look on the bright side: Now you can play golf together.

AFTERWORD

WHAT DID YOU EXPECT?

Now you're on your own.

You've read *What to Expect When Your Wife Is Expanding*, you've studied the advice and information, you've looked up the hard words. You have devoted time and energy to preparing yourself for the dawn of fatherhood. Well done. Without intelligent, devoted readers like you, a money-making sequel would be impossible.

We have made every effort to be absolutely complete in our coverage of the issues and possibilities of pregnancy. We feel certain that answers to all your questions lie in these pages. Although we just realized that we forgot to write up that piece on taking a nonstress test—don't worry, there's nothing to it, really. Oh shoot, we didn't say anything about prepregnancy genetic counseling or choosing a godparent either. Suppose it's a little late now. And we fully intended to provide a thorough discussion of the pros and cons of cesarean births from the father's perspective, but you can figure it out for yourselves. We did mention Montgomery's tubercles, didn't we? Pretty sure we did. And bonding? We didn't do bonding either? Well, it's important, so do it, and that's all you really need to know. Listen, maybe it wouldn't be such a bad idea to get ahold of some *other* guidebook to pregnancy, just sort of as a way to double-check. Oh shoot, we definitely should have done that feature on emergency delivery when you don't get to the hospital on time.

Dads-to-be, just remember this: You can be pregnant and funny, but a hysterical pregnancy is no pregnancy at all. We're not sure what that means. But if you just remember it, maybe it'll keep you from worrying about other things too much.

Have a great pregnancy, a wonderful outcome—oh, and give our best to your wife.

RECOMMENDED READING

Suzanne Arms, *Immaculate Deception.* Houghton-Mifflin, 1975.

T. Berry Brazelton, *Infants & Mothers.* Delacorte, 1969.

Hal Cannon, ed., *Cowboy Poetry: A Gathering.* Gibbs M. Smith, 1985.

Bennett Cerf, *Riddle-De-Dee.* Ballantine, 1962.

Grantley Dick-Read, *Childbirth Without Fear.* Harper & Row, 1972.

M. Eiger and S.W. Olds, *The Complete Book of Breastfeeding.* Bantam, 1973.

Arlene Eisenberg, Heidi Eisenberg Murkoff, and Sandee Eisenberg Hathaway, R.N., *What to Expect When You're Expecting.* Workman Publishing, 1984.

Sheila Kitzinger, *The Complete Book of Pregnancy & Childbirth.* Alfred A. Knopf, 1986.

Dorothy Kunhardt, *Pat the Bunny.* Western Publishing, 1991.

P. Leach, *Your Baby & Child.* Alfred A. Knopf, 1978.

Frederick Leboyer, *Birth Without Violence.* Alfred A. Knopf, 1975.

A.J. Liebling, *The Sweet Science.* Penguin, 1951.

Irwin Steig, *Poker for Fun & Profit.* Astor-Honor, 1959.

Brian Walker, ed., *The Best of Ernie Bushmiller's Nancy.* Henry Holt & Company, 1988.

Ethel H. Weddle, *Walter Chrysler: Boy Machinist.* Childhood of Famous Americans Series. Bobbs-Merrill, 1960.